Cabbage Heart

CABBAGE HEART

by

Martin Ramsay

Narrow Gate House Publishers

Cabbage Heart
Copyright © 2023
Martin L. Ramsay

Version 1.0 — May, 2023
Version 1.1 — June, 2023
Version 1.2 — July, 2023

Cover design by Narrow Gate House Publishers, Berea, KY
Cover photos by Martin and Charlie Ramsay

All rights reserved. No part of this publication may be reproduced, stored in a retrieval system, or transmitted in any form or by any means—electronic, mechanical, photocopying, recording, or otherwise—without prior written permission of the publisher. The only exception is brief quotations in printed reviews.

Published by Narrow Gate House Publishers
PO Box 483
Berea, Kentucky 40403-0483
www.narrowgatehouse.com

Narrow Gate House Publishers is the publication division of CEATH Company, www.ceath.com.

ISBN # 978-1-941099-17-9
Library of Congress Preassigned Control Number: 9781941099179

Dedication

to
all the doctors, nurses, physician assistants, respiratory therapists,
physical therapists, housekeepers, dietitians and other professionals
who supported me in my recovery

to
my beloved wife
Charlie
without whom I would not be the man I am today

to
Jesus Christ
who holds my life in His hands

Table of Contents

Prologue 3

Success I 5

Perspective 11

Success II 17

Yellowstone 21

Blockage 27

Jolt 35

Surgeon 39

Preparation 45

Surgery 57

Unit 61

Hospital 73

Recovery 87

Opportunity 99

Prologue

"I'm sorry. I did find a blockage, in fact several of them, but I couldn't fix them with a stent. You're going to need open heart surgery and you need it soon."

Apparently my reaction did not demonstrate that I appreciated the gravity of my situation. The doctor tried again.

"This is serious. You're going to need six bypasses on your heart. I need to schedule you with a thoracic surgeon as quickly as possible, hopefully this week."

"Uh huh." My response was still rather tepid.

In my defense I had just been through a heart catheterization procedure performed by Dr. Cook. Prior to this I had been a reasonably healthy 66 year old man. There had been some concern that I might have a small blockage in a coronary artery. The doctor had said, "Most likely we can correct it during the procedure with a stent. I'm usually right about these things, but occasionally I do get surprised …". Apparently what he saw had surprised, even alarmed him. But it wasn't sinking in for me. The drug I'd been given during the heart catheterization procedure still had me under its influence and nothing was going to perturb me.

Dr. Cook gave up trying to get me to understand and went in search of my wife to explain the situation to her.

Three weeks ago I had major open heart surgery. It was completely unexpected. A little over four weeks ago I had no inkling that there might even be a problem with my heart, let alone that such major invasive surgery might be required. My world has been turned upside down. Yet here I am, recovering from six, count them, six bypasses around what I had always thought was a relatively healthy organ.

I'm still processing what has happened to me and I'm still looking at many more weeks, perhaps months, of recovery.

My cherished hope is that, by recounting what happened to me in this small volume, I might be of some assistance to you, should you or someone you love be faced with major surgery, or a new and dire diagnosis, or an unexpected major life change. Perhaps my story will be helpful to you as you face the serious twists and turns that life seems to throw at us.

Success I

Every person has their unique story. There is no such thing as the average person or even the typical person; there are only real individuals. We have each been shaped by the events in our lives and the nuances of our reactions to those events. This is my story.

In 1975 Charlie and I got married. Charlie is a fabulous redhead from Tennessee, a strong woman with an interesting nickname. Her parents and people that knew her as a little girl call her Earlean, but anyone who knew her from seventh grade on calls her Charlie.

At age 17 I had come to Berea College in Kentucky from North Carolina. Charlie and I met in college, fell deeply in love, and tied the knot in an outdoor ceremony. Charlie was 20; I had just turned 19. (When Charlie told her mother that I was younger than her by a year and a half, her mother said, "What are you doing? Taking one to raise?")

It was a glorious time. We lived in a tiny, shabby apartment and survived on love and Charlie's income as a nurse's aide at the hospital. She quit school so I could finish my bachelor's degree in Chemistry.

It was a time of heartache, too. We lost our first baby to a miscarriage. But soon Mark came along. By now I had graduated and was working at the hospital myself, in the lab, drawing blood and counting white blood cells. We agreed that Charlie would stay home with the baby and I would now earn the living. If I worked overtime and pulled call, I could just about bring in $9,000 in a year.

Luke came next and we were soon hankering for a place of our own. We found five acres that had a ratty old mobile home on it — two bedrooms, one no bigger than a closet, and one bath. There were abandoned junk cars in the woods and a hole in the ground the previous owner had used for a garbage dump. It was a mess, but it was ours and we could see what it might become. We moved in on April Fool's Day 1980.

We spent the next two years building on to the the trailer, pouring a foundation around it, adding a bedroom and porch on the front, and putting a roof over the whole thing. When it was done we had just over 800 square feet. We got the junk cars towed away and the garbage dump filled in.

I was fortunate to get a job as a systems analyst at Hyster, a local manufacturing company. The position had nothing to do with my chemistry degree, but I discovered I loved programming, systems design, and seeing my ideas actually help people do their jobs. I had some inspirational bosses and colleagues. Work-wise, I felt like I had finally found my calling.

John Paul arrived next and, a couple of years later, we were expecting our fourth child. Charlie said there wasn't a drawer to put the baby in. We had considered trying to buy a bigger house, but a neighbor suggested we build on our own five acres, and that's what we did.

Sunday afternoons while Charlie rested and her middle expanded week after week, we would sketch out the house we would build. It wasn't fancy — we could't afford fancy — but it had four bedrooms and two baths and the hallway was bigger than the trailer's two foot wide passageway. We found a builder who said he could build it off of our sketches. We cut corners where we could, using discontinued lighting fixtures from Lowes and trim wood that had joints. By the time Joseph arrived — our fourth boy — the house was under construction and we were able to move in when he was just a few months old.

I had an opportunity to take a job with a competitor to Hyster, Clark Material Handling. It meant a substantial pay raise, but I would have to drive to Lexington every day. The commute was about an hour, more if there was heavy traffic or if parking was hard to find downtown. I started out doing a major manufacturing software installation. When that project finished, I took a position as Director of Training and Development reporting to the Vice President for Human Resources. I found I liked that work as well. I was able to leverage my technical expertise to teach just-in-time manufacturing and lots of software topics, but I also learned and taught topics like effective meetings and self-directed work teams.

In 1993 Clark Material Handling was purchased by a company called Terex. Terex used some of Clark's cash to meet other obligations and the company I worked for began finding itself in difficulty. The layoffs began in earnest during the summer and my job changed to coordinating outplacement services for newly unemployed former colleagues. The idea was to help these people learn to write good resumes and to find their next job. Then my boss called me into his office. It was November and I, too, was being let go. Unfortunately, by the time I was being shown the door, there was no money left for outplacement, or for severance pay. I got a check for two weeks pay and a pat on the back. That was it.

So there I was, the sole breadwinner of a family of six, with the oldest now a junior in high school already thinking about college. The two week check would cover the mortgage for one more month and then we were going to be in deep trouble.

I had some interest from a software company in Atlanta. We drove down as a family to check it out. I think the job might have been good, but Charlie and I just could not see uprooting the boys, taking them from the community where they had friends and school, leaving the house we had built, and pulling up the deep roots we had established. I passed on the job and decided, instead, that I would try to make a go of it as a self-employed person.

We cleared off the dining room table and called it "Daddy's office". The children were instructed not to answer the phone during the day. And I started looking for work. People ask me what I do and, not so tongue in cheek, I reply, "Anything for money." When you're unemployed, you'll do just about anything to bring in a dollar and put food on the table.

One of the last projects I had been involved in before being laid off was to help another Terex facility with a software implementation. That project was well under way when I got the pink slip. I now called my contact at that facility in Mississippi and informed him that I wasn't going to be able to complete the project. He was upset. "We were counting on you. We don't have your kind of expertise at our facility. We really need you!" I waited. "Isn't there something we can do?" he asked. I proposed that perhaps I could work as an outside consultant instead of as an employee of the Terex empire. He jumped on the idea and I heaved a sigh of relief. My first client had materialized.

Those first two years were really tough. Charlie and I had a deal: If I ever could't "make payroll" (translation: write Charlie a check to cover the mortgage and food), I would have to go get a "real job." It was very close several times, but I managed to avoid becoming a traditional employee again.

Over the years my network of contacts and the projects I was invited to work on grew. We called our company CEATH Company — an inside joke from our college days when my cousin John and his wife Eileen had thought we'd start a company together. CEATH stood for "Charlie, Eileen, and their husbands." In 1999 we incorporated CEATH Company with Charlie and me as equal shareholders. We gave Charlie the title of Vice President of Finance because, as she said, "Martin brings in the money and I spend it wisely." I ended up doing projects for many well-known companies all over the country and then, through my contacts at General Motors and Saturn, going international. So far I've worked in 13 different countries on four continents.

During that time, one by one, the boys went off to college. The older three found wonderful women who thought they would make good husbands. They all settled within ten miles of our house while Joseph went off to UCLA to pursue a career in geophysics. He still lives in Los Angeles. Between the three local families there are now 13 grandchildren. And I kept puttering away at being self employed and working under the CEATH Company banner.

During the last fifteen years or so I had been focusing more and more on building recurring business. Project work is fine and a lot of fun, but you always have to be hunting the next job. If I could build work that was more of a subscription, I would be able to bring in income without having to market quite so hard.

The most successful of those endeavors was the LAMP Consortium. My vision was that members of the consortium could subscribe to services related to technology for education. I first signed up several colleges who were using the software and services to enhance their on-campus courses. Long before distance education became a thing, students could access reading material, turn in assignments, check their grades and much more from their dorm room or off campus. It was a way to extend the classroom in time and space, from a specific room three days a week to anytime, anywhere.

The idea began to take off. Soon schools were using LAMP Consortium services to offer true distance education courses where you didn't have to come to a specific location. And then I started getting interest from organizations that weren't colleges, but that had something they wanted to teach. Non-profits wanted to reach their constituents, associations wanted to reach their members, for-profit organizations wanted to reach their employees and their customers.

When the pandemic hit in 2020, suddenly everyone wanted what the LAMP Consortium was offering. It may be a bit crass, but COVID was good for business. We knew how to help people who suddenly needed to reach people at a distance, and we could do it quickly and inexpensively.

As I began to think about the fact that I wasn't getting any younger, I began to explore ways I could bring others into the business. I had no intention of retiring. In fact, one of the benefits of being self employed is that there is no one to tell you you have to go from working full time to stopping cold. Instead of my work volume falling off a cliff, from full time to nothing, I had the luxury of just dialing back a bit, taking fewer projects and gradually easing toward partial retirement.

The problem was the LAMP Consortium. With all of the subscribers — there are over 30 as of this writing — I couldn't just begin dialing back. I needed help.

In June of 2021 the former CFO of one of the LAMP Consortium members, Jeremy Anderson, asked if we could have lunch. He was leaving his employer to come and help his brother-in-law who had been called as the pastor of a small, struggling church in rural Kentucky. He was also going to help out at his brother-in-law's hardware store. During our lunch we discussed the pros and cons of being self-employed and considered possible lines of work that Jeremy might find open to him.

Something prompted me to ask Jeremy if he would like to work for the LAMP Consortium. After a couple of months of discussions, Jeremy came to work with me on a part-time basis. He would work at the hardware store three days a week, while on Thursdays and Fridays he would work for the LAMP Consortium. After nearly 30 years of working mostly on my own, it was nice to have a colleague. We could discuss strategy, grumble about demanding clients, or just have a conversation between two people who actually understood the business.

As I reflect on my career, I'm reminded of a friend of mine who once said that he appreciates being able to eat indoors. When I asked him what he meant by "eat indoors" he said, "You know. I like to have food on the table and a roof over my head. Anything more than that is extra." I realized I had adopted the "eat indoors" philosophy years ago.

By all accounts, I've been a success. My family never starved. Charlie and I aren't rich by most people's standards, but we're comfortable enough. Our house and cars are paid for. We have four wonderful sons, three daughters-in-law, and thirteen grandkids that we love and who love us.

There are some people who might criticize and say that I should have built a bigger business, employing a dozen consultants and expanding into other markets. I might have been able to do that, but that had never been my goal. Since being laid off in 1993, I've seen it as my mission to just make a living, to allow us to "eat indoors."

Also, financial success is not the only measure of success.

Perspective

When Charlie and I got married, I wasn't sure that there was a God. I had no understanding that would point to His existence, let alone any experience that would indicate that he was real and personal to me. How that all changed is an important part of this story.

The summer before Charlie and I got married, I was able to make several trips to Tennessee to visit her at her parent's home. On Sundays, Charlie's mother insisted we go to church. It was a small country Baptist church and I wasn't thrilled about attending. I had very few experiences with church and thought I probably didn't need or want another one.

My parents, probably thinking they were doing me a favor, had provided very little in the way of religious guidance. When we had occasionally gone to church when I was younger, it was to a Quaker "meeting." Quakers don't have a church service, they have a meeting which consists of people sitting in a circle, I learned later, waiting for the Spirit to speak through one of them. To my recollection, the Spirit never did.

Later, when my grandmother came to live with us after her Methodist pastor husband, my grandfather, had passed away, my mother would occasionally drive her mother to a Methodist church to attend a worship service. I was a reluctant passenger.

So when Charlie's mom announced we were going to church, I was ambivalent. But there was this redhead that I was sweet on and she was going, so I went.

The Spirit never spoke at any Quaker meeting I attended, but that was not the case at this little Baptist church. The Spirit spoke, and spoke often. Two of the Holy Spirit's main recipients were two middle aged women named May and Lois. Whether it was deliberate or purely coincidental remains a controversy to this day, but Charlie's mom chose a pew right in front of May and Lois. We were seated and the service began with singing.

People at that church knew how to sing, and they knew how to praise the Lord, and, yes, they knew how to listen to the Holy Spirit. It wasn't long before May and Lois were shouting "Amen" and "Hallelujah" and "Praise the Lord." Hymn books started flying and I was ducking down in the pew. This guy with very little church experience was frightened and fascinated at the same time. I'd never been a part of something like this. One thing was for sure: this was not fake. This was the real deal. And for the first time in my life I began to wonder if perhaps God might be real after all; I'd just never been exposed to Him before.

That began a great searching in me. I'd like to say that the matter was resolved quickly and efficiently. It was not. I went through several phases.

※

I was what was known as a "good kid." I did well in school (mostly A's in high school, only one B in college) and had, in fact, skipped my senior year to go to college at age seventeen. I had never given my parents any trouble. And, as a result, I held myself in rather high esteem. I truly believed I was good and I figured that almost everyone would have agreed with me.

But God needed to show me how wrong I was. Through a series of incidents, I became increasingly aware of my inner failings. God showed me that, even though I thought of myself as a rule-follower, I was willing to lie when it suited me. God showed me that, even though I thought of myself as kind and helpful, I held on to malice toward people I believed had wronged me. God showed me that my high opinion of myself was actually the ugly sin of arrogance.

One night I remember lying on my back on the college soccer field looking up at the stars and calling out to God, "If You are real, show me." With tears in my eyes, I realized how far, far away I was from God.

God did begin showing Himself. I loved being outdoors, loved the mountains, loved the turn of the seasons and the beauty in nature. I began to see the thumbprint of God in these things. I remember that winter going out walking one evening. There had been a fairly good snowfall during the day and I reveled in slogging through the deep snow out in the open fields that night. The clouds were gone and in their place was a chilled silence, so quiet you could almost hear the twinkle of the stars. The beauty of that night took my breath away. And I could almost hear God whisper, "Yes, I am real. Look around you; I made all of this. Yes, I love you. You are precious to Me. Yes, I want you to believe in Me. I want you to get to know Me."

By the time I was in college personal integrity had become very important to me. Some of that may have come from my parents. My mother had dedicated her life to raising my brother and me. My dad's father believed strongly in workers' rights and had spent his life working for the labor movement. He and my grandmother had been heavily involved in the civil rights movement, working with Dr. Martin Luther King and others. My dad's belief in pacifism had led him to declare himself a contentious objector during the Korean War.

I remember being on a date with Charlie and telling her, "I will never leave you." As I said those words, I realized I had made a commitment to her, one that I would now not willingly break if I could possibly avoid it. I had come to believe that, if a person did make a commitment, they had jolly well better do everything in their power to keep it. If a person didn't intend to keep a commitment, or didn't know if they could or would, it was better not to make the commitment at all.

If something was true, it was worth pursuing that truth wherever it led. If something wasn't true, it may be amusing or of passing interest, but it was not worth dedicating one's life to. "I will never leave you" grew into the commitment that can only develop between a man and a woman who are married to each other. When Charlie and I said, "I do, 'till death do us part" it was not a commitment either one of us took lightly. I meant what I said then, and I still do.

It was against this backdrop that Charlie and I were now married and living in our little apartment. At her gentle suggestion, we started attending church. Not with any regularity, I'm sorry to say, but I was beginning to hear some biblical teaching for the first time in my life. What I learned began to make sense. I was beginning to understand some things that felt like they really were true, like they were worth dedicating my life to.

One thing I struggled with was the disconnect between things I saw happening in the world. On one hand there was the natural beauty and perfect order of the outdoors that I loved so much. Growing up in western North Carolina, I had a profound respect for the complex design of nature. My spirit responded at a deep level to the majesty of the tall mountains, to the teeming life in a mountain stream, to the turn of the seasons and the rightness of everything. As a child I spent many happy hours roaming the hills and creeks of our rural home.

Yet that same world was clearly flawed and broken. This was the era of psychedelic drug use, of the Kennedy and King assassinations, of the Vietnam war, of Richard Nixon, of hippies and Woodstock. It seemed that people were trying to tear the world apart at the seams and they didn't really have anything better with which to replace it. How could this be? How could the world be both beautiful and perfect while simultaneously terrifying and cruel?

In church, I heard for the first time, a plausible explanation coming from the Bible. The preachers were clear on the biblical perspective: the world had once been a perfect place. God had created it so. Everything I knew from personal experience about the natural world was correct. Yet God had also created human beings with the capacity to make choices. He hadn't created a race of robots who would slavishly obey Him, but people with the free will to chose Him, or to reject Him. Unfortunately, as the Bible described, human beings chose wrongly, preferring their own selfish desires over God's love for them.

The preachers I listened to give this rejection of God a name: sin. Our choice, as human beings, had pushed God away and now we found ourselves separated and wandering far away from Him, lost in our own arrogance and desires. Sin was more than doing something wrong; sin, according to the Bible, was a state of being, a state of brokenness that completely mars our ability to see things clearly.

This made so much sense to me. It precisely matched the evidence I confronted every day, whether contemplating a leaf or being inundated by the tragedies on the nightly news. It confirmed what I knew to be true about myself that night, lying in the soccer field and being overwhelmed with my estrangement from God. It confirmed what I saw in the world: wars, man's inhumanity to man, the cruelty that seems to lurk, just out of sight, in each of us.

If this was a true explanation of why the world is the way it is, what was to be done? How could a man who was lost and far away from God be reconciled to the same God who loved him and earnestly desired to have him back?

The Bible had an answer for that as well.

We know experientially that choices have consequences; the Bible confirms this. The choice that is inherent at the core of our being is that we have all turned our backs on God, and that choice has consequences: it means we will all die. The Bible tells us that one of the consequences of sin is death. Another is separation from God. And yet that is not what He desires; He loves us and, even though we are completely lost and separated from Him, He desires to restore our relationship to Him.

He desires us to make a different choice, to choose to return to Him.

But for God to say, "Oh, never mind. I was only kidding about the consequences." would be completely contrary to His character. He is perfectly righteous; even though He loves us, there must be consequences to our turning our back on Him. So He made a way. He provided a substitute, a perfect replacement who would take what we deserve in our place. That Someone would take our punishment and offer that substitution to us. All we have to do is accept that gift.

The Someone is Jesus, God the Son who came to live on earth and to take the punishment we deserve in our place. Jesus was called, among other things, Emmanuel, which means "God with us." Jesus is God, the God who loves us enough to come and suffer in our place. Jesus said, "I and the Father are one." (John 10:30). He also said, "No one comes to the Father except through me." (John 14:6) I became convinced that Jesus is, indeed, the way, the only way, back to God.

God further showed that Jesus is the Son of God by, after He had been killed on a cross and buried, raising Him from the dead. If we knew where to look, we could find the bones of all of the heads of the other major religions of the world: Buddha, Confucius, Mohammad, Moses, and so on. Not so Jesus. As the angels said on the morning Jesus was resurrected from the dead, "Why are you looking for the living among the dead? He is not here." (Luke 24:5). By His resurrection, God proved that Jesus has the power to overcome death and is a perfect substitute for the punishment we deserve. The consequences of our sin is death, but Jesus had overcome both sin and death.

This gift of Jesus is what we call the Gospel — the "good news" that no longer do we need to wander lost and estranged from God. Through Jesus, we can be reconciled to God. We do not have to permanently die, but can have eternal life. The Bible promises that if we will believe in Jesus, and that He paid for the punishment that we deserved, and if we will "confess with our mouth" (in other words, be willing to publicly put our belief into words), we can be saved — I could be saved — from the terrible lostness I had been experiencing. (Romans 10:9-10)

I would like to say that my understanding of this came quickly and easily. It did not. Even after I had decided I would, as we say, make a public confession of my new faith in Jesus, it took me many years to understand what the Bible had to say about God, about Jesus, about the human condition, about my status, about how to live. But the more I read the Bible, the more I found its statements to be absolutely true. Even reading the same passage again later would often reveal a deeper truth that I had missed before.

The more I explored the Bible, the more I saw that it withstood all challenges. Many have said that a certain historical account in the Bible could not be true, only to have archeologists discover proof in the desert that the account was spot on. Many say the Bible is a dusty, obsolete book with no relevance today. I have not found that to be the case; the Bible is as relevant to me today as it had been when its various parts were written. The Bible need never fear science or archeology or history. If something in the Bible doesn't seem right, the problem isn't with the Bible. The problem is with my understanding. Perhaps I need to learn more, or need to be more patient, or need to pray for God to reveal to me the proper understanding of a passage.

As my faith grew, I realized another important fact. This trustworthiness of the Bible meant that it could become the absolute standard by which all actions and behavior could be compared. I had become increasingly concerned at the way that, left to their own devices, human beings would change their mind again and again about what was right. I had begun to study history and I realized more and more how much of a mess people make of things. If the prevailing wisdom today is going to be thrown out tomorrow in favor of something different, it meant that there could be nothing that was really true, nothing that was stable, never anything that could be said to be truly right or wrong.

Those with a different view would say that humanity is always evolving, always getting better, always becoming more enlightened. It doesn't take long, looking at the history of humanity, to realize what a flimsy perspective this is. Humanity may be getting better in one regard, and yet there is another war, another bombing, another killing, another example of man's inhumanity to man. No, humanity is not getting better; humanity has, almost from the beginning, been lost, broken, and estranged from God. The Bible has it right. All other approaches are like castles in the air with no foundation, like houses built on quicksand.

In the first chapter I gave you a brief history of my life up to this point with the kinds of details most people might be curious about. Where did I live? What did I do for a living? Was I married? Did I have a family? What obstacles had I overcome? Had I been successful?

This chapter has provided a much more personal description of my perspective about things that matter even more deeply than "success." What do I know to be true about God? What has been my experience with Jesus? Why is the world the way it is? What does the Bible say about these deep questions we all, in our more honest moments, wonder about? Can the Bible be trusted?

My earnest conviction is that I (and you as well) was lost and estranged from God. Yet I have placed my faith in Jesus and what He did for me on the cross. I now have an eternal perspective: this life is not the end and this world is only a temporary dwelling place. The Bible provides vital information, revealed from God, about this and so much more, and it is absolutely true and trustworthy.

Success II

Given the perspective of the previous chapter, please allow me to revisit the idea of success.

After many years of seeking and getting to know God better, I came to understand that a definition of success that is based on material wealth, job accomplishments, number and stature of friends, or anything like that, is a weak definition. Instead I began to have a more long-term view, some would even say an eternal view, of success.

A good friend of mine, a Messianic Jew named Rod Eisenberg, once told me that the Jewish definition of success is different from the common understanding. This intrigued me and I asked Rod to explain. He pointed out that Jewish history is full of examples of ways in which the Jews had attempted to amass wealth or standing, but that these things were often taken away, often by force. I knew enough about history, the Spanish Inquisition and the Holocaust for example, to know that this was true. Instead, Rod explained, a Jew measures his success by the degree to which his grandchildren establish godly homes. Rod explained that, if your grandchildren establish homes that are focused on the Most High, it means that your godly influence has carried beyond the children you raised to households you did not so directly influence.

I liked that definition, and found it resonating with my own. My success was not measured in the size of my IRA investments, even though I had attempted to diligently put aside money each year for the day when I would be less able to work. My success was not measured in the size and profitability of the business I had built, even though I had been able to do so in some measure. My success was not measured in the number and stature of the friends I had made through the years, even though my virtual Rolodex was bursting with a network of friends and business associates I had accumulated in working across the globe. My success was not even measured in the fact that I had been married and faithful to Charlie for 47 years, even though she is my best friend, my confidant, and the most desirable woman I know.

Instead, I needed to look at success a different way. I needed to have the eternal perspective, one that acknowledged that my time here on earth was limited and only a small piece of the whole story. While I am here, I need to be investing in things that matter, things that last. I need to be living a life without regrets, which meant trying not to do wrong and, when I do, to apologize and make it right. I need to be investing in people, not things. I need to be sharing the immense peace and joy I have found in Jesus with others, so that they can experience it too.

For example, I needed to invest in my children and now be investing in my grandchildren. They will long outlive me. I need to be pouring into their lives, keenly interested in what they are doing and how they are growing and maturing, sharing what wisdom I've gained with them.

My definition of success had changed to more closely align with Rod's charming definition. Success for me had become something that was measured with an eternal yardstick, not a temporal one.

I would like to report to you that, once I became a Christian, I immediately started attending a Bible-focused church. Unfortunately, that was not the case. Apparently I am a rather slow learner; much of my faith journey has been filled with stumbles and false starts. But I am happy to report that, eventually, I and my family found our way to churches where God's Word is preached and where people love each other as the Bible instructs us to.

In 1998 we eventually landed in a little country church called Pilot Knob Missionary Baptist Church. When we started attending Pilot Knob, the congregation numbered approximately 40 people on a Sunday morning. As Charlie and I commented to each other several times in those early years, we didn't know hardly anyone who attended Pilot Knob and we really didn't have much in common with any of them. We live in a small town, one where people get to know each other. We found it odd that these were not people we had interacted with in some way before, whether it was at a PTA meeting or shopping at Walmart. But, over the years, we came to love these fellow church-goers. We loved the diversity of backgrounds, socioeconomic standings, and ages. Despite the diversity, these were people held together by their shared love of Jesus and respect for God's Word.

When we started attending Pilot Knob, once you were graduated from high school and no longer a part of the children's Sunday School program, you had two choices for Sunday School: the men's class or the women's class. I had great joy attending the men's class with my sons who were, by now, mostly out of high school. But the pastor at the time, Bob Taylor, asked me if I would be willing to try to start a couple's Sunday School class.

I was willing, although conscious of the high responsibility I'd been given. The first Sunday we tried holding the couple's class was comprised of eight people: Charlie and me and three other couples.

Today my Sunday School class has between 30 and 40 on a Sunday morning. And Pilot Knob has grown as well, with a rich variety of Sunday School classes going on. We now have two worship services, the early 8:00 AM service and the traditional 10:45 service. The combined total attendance on Sunday mornings at Pilot Knob is around 240. And a full 75% of worship service attendees also attend Sunday School.

Even though my role in this has been quite small, I feel that the number of people being influenced by Biblical teaching and worshiping together in a close-knit community of fellow believers looms large in any meaningful definition of success.

In my Sunday School class I chose a curriculum that, over an eight year cycle, covers all 66 books of the Bible. I like that. All of the Bible is there for a reason, both the well-known books and the obscure ones. By teaching a cycle of the books of the Bible, I was exposing people (and myself) to the entire canon.

As I write this, I am in my third eight-year cycle. I've kept all my lesson notes from previous years; those three ring binders of messy, hand-written lesson plans are part of my legacy.

Occasionally I would take a break and teach a series that I thought could be helpful. I did one on Hebrew History because I found that people did not understand the sweep of history in the Old Testament very well. I taught a series on how we got the Bible. This one was particularly important to me personally; I've learned that, if I want to understand something well, I need to prepare to teach it to others. I wanted to know the history of the Bible, and this series called "God Breathed" allowed me to dig deeply into exotic topics like the Septuagint, the Vulgate, the Essenes, and how the scriptural canon was settled.

I even did a series on other religions, starting with our own Baptist faith, moving more broadly into Protestant and Catholic faiths, and ending with Judaism, Islam, Hinduism, Buddhism, more modern cults and even the religion of secular humanism.

More recently, our current pastor Greg Lakes asked me if I would consider focusing more on discipleship. In other words, he would like me to help people put their understanding of the Bible into practical action as they grow in their faith. I told him that, in the past, I wouldn't have trusted myself to do that. I feared my ego might run away with me and I would stray from what God would have us to know into what Martin Ramsay thought was important or entertaining. Pastor Greg assured me that he thought I was mature enough in my faith by now to tackle this new assignment, so I've been working on that for the past year or so.

The current series tackles many of the issues in our modern world that seem to be so confusing to people. We've considered gender, race, origins, marriage, and more, helping people gain a Biblical perspective on topics that seem so convoluted and controversial, if all one had to listen to was to social media and cable news.

I say all this not to brag but to highlight this different definition of success that has come to seep through my very soul. What I do with my time here on earth matters to me. What better could I be doing than studying the Bible to develop Sunday School material to help people grow stronger in their faith? What better could I be doing that investing in the lives of my 13 grandchildren?

For example, it has become a tradition that the entire Ramsay clan gathers on Sundays at our house after church for lunch. The amazing Charlie typically prepares lunch for 21 people (even my 94 year old mother often attends). The fellowship of family around the dinner table is a precious investment that I see paying eternal dividends.

Things like that are the real components of success.

Yellowstone

Early in my efforts to get CEATH Company up and running, I had received a call from a friend I had made through the American Production and Inventory Control Society. Ben said he wanted me to facilitate a day long off-site strategic planning meeting of his board of directors. That was work I thought I could do well; I had been trained as a facilitator while working for Clark Equipment and had facilitated many meetings related to strategic planning.

"There's just one problem," Ben said. "I'm afraid we can't pay you for that work."

Whoa, I thought. *That's not good. I'm trying to make a living. I'm trying to eat indoors and cut Charlie that "paycheck" at the end of each month. Working for free is not what I need to be doing.*

"I still think you'll do the meeting, though," said Ben. *Oh really? And why in the world would you think that, Ben?* "Because we will pay your travel expenses, and the meeting is going to be in Hawaii."

Well, that was a little different. I'd never been to Hawaii and thought it would be nice to have a little time there, especially if someone else was paying the tab. Ben knew Charlie and suggested she might like to come along. I had been bumped off a flight earlier and had been given a voucher for a free flight. I was able to use that to purchase a ticket for Charlie for very little money. The rest of the expenses would be covered by Ben's organization. Even though I didn't make any money out of the deal, Charlie and I did go to Hawaii and had a great time.

That was the beginning of a goal for us: to visit all 50 states together. We perceived that Hawaii and Alaska would be the most difficult two states, and we already had Hawaii checked off. We set two rules for our quest. First, we had to go together. It didn't count if I had been to a state doing client work if Charlie didn't come along. Second, we had to spend quality time there. It didn't count if we just changed planes in the state (as we had done in California on the trip to Hawaii). I started tracking which states we had visited and realized we had already been to quite a few. We began deliberately looking for opportunities to visit the remaining states. Travel to a conference in Phoenix was expanded to take a driving trip through California, Nevada and Utah. Work for the Wyoming Community College system was expanded to take in Montana, North Dakota and South Dakota. Charlie suggested we go to Alaska for our 40th wedding anniversary. By 2022 we had visited all but five states: Oregon, Idaho, Minnesota, Connecticut and Rhode Island.

A Christmas card from friends who lived in Boise invited us to stop by if we were ever out west. We had always wanted to take a driving trip to the west coast, and this seemed like the incentive we needed. We began planning a three week trip that would take us to visit friends in Iowa, to the headwaters of the Mississippi in Minnesota, across North Dakota to take in the Theodore Roosevelt national park, through Wyoming to Yellowstone where our friends would meet us, then on to their home in Boise and on to Oregon and the California redwoods before heading back east. The trip would take in three of our five missing states.

Because Jeremy Anderson was working for the LAMP Consortium two days a week, this would be possible. Jeremy would keep an eye on things and let me have the first break I'd had in a very long time.

We had a wonderful trip, stopping frequently to see unusual things or natural beauty. We often took back roads rather than the interstate to get a sense of the people and the culture of an area. And we certainly enjoyed our time in Yellowstone with our friends from Boise.

There was a slight worry, however. In Yellowstone, I found I would get short of breath occasionally, even feeling a bit tight in my chest. I chalked it up to the altitude; Yellowstone is at 7,000 feet or more. I mostly ignored it, figuring I would worry about it later.

Later Charlie would remind me that I had been getting a little short of breath even before our trip. She pointed out I would sometimes be panting a bit when I came up the stairs from my office in the basement.

Earlier that year I had begun walking three days a week with my cousin John (husband of Eileen, the "E" in CEATH) who had retired and come back to live in Berea We would meet at 7:00 AM and walk for about three miles. I really enjoyed that. We watched the sun come up and got our blood pumping a bit while having a nice chat as we walked.

I've never been athletic and certainly would never characterize myself as an athlete. That honor goes to my brother. He was always throwing, kicking or hitting a ball. I was lucky if I could connect a bat with anything. At recess I was relegated to right field — nobody ever hit anything to right field. At bat I was just hoping for a brief time in the batters box with as little humiliation as possible. My brother and John played soccer, ran track and more in college. I did none of those things.

After college I developed the philosophy that the best exercise was gained organically, doing something that was productive or useful. I enjoyed gardening; the exercise of hoeing a row of corn felt good. I chopped wood in the fall to feed the wood stove in our basement. I worked with our goats to keep them healthy and to put up hay to feed them in the winter. The walks with John didn't quite fit the definition of "productive" but they were pleasant and a great way to start the day.

Every once in a while, during our walks, if I were honest with myself, I would feel the occasional twinge of shortness of breath. I chalked it up to aging. A nurse later told Charlie she guessed we both had assumed that I was just getting old and fat. That was closer to the truth than I might have liked to admit.

When we got home from the trip out west I had my regular annual physical. This was with a new doctor, Dr. Dustin Devers. Earlier my regular doctor had suddenly left his practice because of "family issues." I needed to get established, preferably with a younger doctor who was settled and who wasn't going to retire before I no longer needed him or her. Dr. Devers had come recommended, so I had made an appointment to get established with him as soon as we got back from our trip out west.

I liked Dr. Devers very much. He was everything I had hoped for. Young, but not too young. An excellent listener. Not someone who assumed the solution to every problem was inside a pill bottle. We got to know each other. He listened, poked and prodded. He asked if I had any specific problems. I really didn't have much to report. Generally I'm reasonably healthy for a man my age. Yes, I could shed a few pounds. Maybe my exercise regimen could be beefed up. But overall, medical people told me I was doing fairly well. I did mention the shortness of breath at 7,000 feet in Yellowstone.

"Tell me more about that," said Dr. Devers.

I explained the feeling I had experienced on our trip out west.

"Do you feel anything like that at other times?"

"No, not really. Well, sometimes when I'm walking and trying to talk at the same time I may feel a twinge in my chest. It's nothing, really."

Dr. Devers wondered if I'd be interested in doing a stress test. A stress test involved having EKG leads on your chest while you walked on a treadmill as the speed increased. "At your age, it would be a good idea to get a baseline measurement." I was willing, so Dr. Devers sent me to Dr. Scott Cook, a cardiologist in Richmond.

I liked Dr. Cook as well. He seemed quite eager to tell me not only what he recommended but why he was suggesting it. He listened to my symptoms and said, "I agree with Dr. Devers. I think a stress test would be a good idea. And, just to be thorough, let's get an echocardiogram of your heart. That way we can rule out lots of different potential problems."

The stress test was scheduled. The first time they could get me in was two months out in the middle of July. I promptly forgot about it and went on with life.

Charlie and I flew to a convention in Los Angeles along with our pastor and his wife. Our hotel was a good mile from the conference, so every day we hiked a good distance to the convention center. I felt good about getting the exercise.

Later, in early July, we went to a family reunion in Indiana. In between I was running my business and living life.

On July 14 I reported to Dr. Cook's office for the echocardiogram and stress test. The echocardiogram involved taking off my shirt, lying on my side, and allowing a lovely technician named Camera to use an ultrasound probe to peer into my heart. Camera examined the size and configuration of various parts of my heart, looked carefully at the valves, used doppler technology to measure the blood flow through my heart, all while carrying on a conversation. Camera let me see the screen as she adjusted the probe at different angles. I was fascinated but especially enjoyed our conversation. We talked most about her husband who had died recently from ALS. His last years had been very difficult, but clearly Camera and her late husband were people of strong faith. She was now recovering, and I felt like perhaps she needed someone to hear her story. I wasn't going anywhere and I was glad to listen.

Camera said that, after her husband's disease prevented him from speaking, he would click his tongue if he needed something. One evening she heard him clicking his tongue so she went in to see what he needed. He made her understand that he didn't need anything but was just "praising the Lord for all the ways He was taking care of things."

Camera stopped the probe for a moment. "Even as he was dying, my husband's faith in the Lord's goodness never wavered." Clearly she had the same kind of confidence in God's mercy and care, even now that she was a widow. I had tears in my eyes. Forget the echocardiogram; Camera was a real person with real challenges. I found myself praying for her as she finished up the procedure.

The stress test was run by Elizabeth who placed EKG leads on my chest and had me get on a treadmill. She called in some backup. "Just in case," she said. "People sometimes get a bit woozy so I want a second person making sure you're doing OK while I run the equipment."

I was ready and not nervous. Walking was something I enjoyed and knew how to do. "Our goal," said Elizabeth, "based on a number of factors including your resting heart rate, your age, and so on, is to get your heart rate up to

131 beats per minute. At that speed, we'll be able to see how your heart reacts to being under stress. Ready?" I was, and the treadmill started moving.

I could see my heart rate on the display — it didn't seem to be rising much. "OK," said Elizabeth after about five minutes. "I can see we're going to need to go to phase two with you." The treadmill started moving faster and raised up so that I was walking up hill.

My heart rate increased, but we were still a long way from 131 beats per minute. "We're going to need phase three with you," said Elizabeth. The treadmill started going even faster and now I was walking up a steeper hill.

Again my heart rate increased, but it was only after about 15 minutes of walking that I finally reached the goal. "We can stop now," said Elizabeth, "unless you want to keep going."

"What are the advantages of keeping going?" I asked.

"It will just give the doctor even more information."

"Let's keep going," I said. While I was breathing harder, I wasn't panting or in any kind of distress. I figured since I was already hooked up, getting more data would be sensible.

We kept going until my heart rate reached 141 beats per minutes, ten beats per minute more than the goal. At that point, we agreed that perhaps it was time to call a halt. The treadmill came back down, slowed down, and stopped. Elizabeth helped peel off the EKG lead stickers and I was ready to go home.

On July 21, I was scheduled to come back to see Dr. Cook and get the results of the echocardiogram and the stress test. Dr. Cook was again eager to show me anything I wanted to know about. "The echocardiogram was completely normal," he said. Nothing unusual in the way of configuration of my heart, valves or blood flow. "But I want you to take a look at the stress test," he said.

Dr. Cook explained the five components of an EKG scan. The tracing we're somewhat familiar with starts with a small p wave, then a complex that is called the q,r,s group, followed a little later by a larger t wave. "Notice the segment between the s and t waves," Dr. Cook said. "This is your resting EKG. See how the s-t segment is flat and level?" I did. "That's exactly what we want to see. Now," he said, scrolling down the screen to the next EKG tracing, "This is after you've been walking for five minutes." He pointed to the s-t segment. "Still level," he said. "Flat, just like we want it."

He scrolled down further. "Here we're ten minutes in," he said. "How does it look to you?" he asked.

"It still looks level to me," I said.

"Yes, I agree. Still good." He scrolled down even more. "Here we're at 15 minutes. Still looks pretty good, doesn't it?"

I thought that it did.

"Now, look here." Dr. Cook scrolled down to the very last EKG, the one that had been taken after we'd reached the goal heart rate of 131 beats per minute. "Now what do you see?"

I looked. "Uh, it looks like the s-t segment is kind of low. Lower than it was before."

"It is," he confirmed. "What else do you see?"

"I don't know if it is significant," I said, "but the segment isn't level any more. It kind of goes downhill."

"Right!" agreed Dr. Cook. "This is what we call s-t depression. It is a sign that the heart isn't getting quite as much oxygen as it needs. We're working your heart fairly hard, at this point, and it can't quite recover for the next beat as quickly as it should if it had all the oxygen, all the blood flow, that it requires. This can indicate that there may be some kind of partial blockage." He looked at me to see if I understood.

"Ok, so not a perfect stress test. How bad is it?" I asked.

"We can't say for sure, based on this stress test. It only tells us that there might be a problem. We can treat it with medication and see if that helps. Or we could do what is called a heart catheterization to really see what is going on."

Blockage

I had heard of a hearth cath, but knew very little about it. Dr. Cook proceeded to explain. Under sedation, a tube, called a catheter, is inserted in the patient's artery. Many doctors use the femoral artery in the groin as the point of entry, but Dr. Cook preferred to use one of the branches of the brachial artery in the wrist. "I use the radial artery 95% of the time. It is a smaller artery so there is less risk of bleeding," he explained. The tube is threaded through the artery, moving toward the heart, until it reaches the aorta, the big major artery exiting the heart. Coming off of the aorta are two cardiac arteries that supply the heart with blood. Those arteries are critical to the functioning of the heart.

Using the catheter, a small amount of dye is introduced into the aorta. When the doctor has positioned the catheter just right, the dye will follow the flow of blood into the cardiac arteries. Because the dye is opaque to x-rays, in other words, because the dye will show up on an x-ray, the doctor can get a very good picture of the configuration of the cardiac arteries. The entire heart cath procedure is guided by x-ray imaging. In real time, the doctor can visualize where the catheter is and where the dye is flowing.

"If we find a minor blockage, we can fix it by inserting a stent into the blood vessel." A stent is a small metal tube, sort of like a piece of a soda straw that presses against the walls of the artery where the blockage is found to keep it open. "I'm fairly confident, based on your stress test, that we're dealing with a blockage we can fix with a stent," Dr. Cook said. "Occasionally I get surprised, but not very often. So what do you think? Are you willing to have a heart cath, or do you want to try medication first?"

By now you may have realized that I am someone who thinks things through. I don't like to rush into decisions; I like to weigh the pros and cons. The cons in this case, at least in my mind, were fairly serious. A foreign object would be traveling through my arteries and poking around in my heart. The dye itself could be problematic, Dr. Cook explained. It is a bit hard on the kidneys as they work to filter the foreign chemical out of your blood stream, so he works to minimize the amount of dye used during the procedure. On the other hand, if I did have a problem and the problem could be fixed with a stent, why not go that route?

Charlie and I looked at each other. We have an unwritten rule that we give ourselves a day to think about major decisions. This was certainly a major decision. But both of us, almost at the same time, said, "Maybe we should go ahead and schedule the heart cath."

"That's fine," said Dr. Cook. "If you do think about it and decide you're not ready, you can always call and cancel."

Dr. Cook also gave us some confidence about the facility. The former Pattie A. Clay Hospital in Richmond had undergone a renovation and was now part of the Baptist Health system. During the renovation, a state-of-the-art heart catheterization lab had been installed. "Frankly our heart cath facility is better than any in Lexington," he said. Lexington is the big city about 40 miles up the road. "Many of the Lexington cardiologists schedule their heart cath procedures in our facility," said Dr. Cook, "because they like our set up."

With some trepidation we approached the office of the scheduler to make the appointment. We were delighted to learn that it was Kelly Garrett, a member of our church. A familiar and compassionate face did a lot to calm my nerves. Kelly got me scheduled for a heart cath procedure on July 27, the following Wednesday.

We went home to think and pray. During my Monday walk with cousin John, I talked it over. "I've had two heart cath procedures," he said. I talked to my dad in St. Louis. "I've had three," he reported. Several other people also came forward; apparently the heart cath procedure was more common than I knew.

We both had a sense of peace about the procedure. I had had no trouble except for the occasional shortness of breath, particularly in Yellowstone at high altitudes. But this was my heart we were talking about. It seemed preferable to know what was going on. So, despite the negatives, we reported to the hospital at 8:00 AM on Wednesday morning, July 27.

The two nurses who were assigned to my case were delightful. Charlie and I enjoyed getting to know them as they prepared me for the procedure.

Kelley was from Maryland, a "traveling nurse" who was on temporary assignment in Richmond. She and her husband, and their two dogs, were staying in a travel trailer in a campground in Berea. "Yeah, my husband is a kept man," Kelley laughed. "I go to work and he takes care of the dogs and has supper fixed when I get back to the camper in the evening." When she finished today, however, she was heading back to Maryland to connect with her mother for a trip to Scotland.

Melissa was also a traveling nurse from Poca, West Virginia. I knew the name of the high school sports team in Poca. "Home of the Dots," I quipped.

"That's right!" Melissa was pleased that I'd heard of her small town in West Virginia and of the semi-famous Poca Dots. Melissa had rented an apartment during her assignment in Kentucky. She liked it, but felt that it was a bit expensive and was slightly envious of Kelley's camper situation.

We chatted amiably as they prepared me. The biggest problem came when they tried to get an IV started. I'm sure I was nervous and my veins were hiding. I had to be stuck three times before they finally were able to get the IV line inserted into a vein on my left hand.

Melissa got a phone call and spoke briefly with the caller. After hanging up she looked at me and smiled. "I'll be your bartender today," she announced. Apparently "bartender" is the term the heart cath team uses for the person who will be administering the anesthesia. "You'll be fully awake," she told me. "If you like, you can watch what the doctor is doing on the big screen TV. I'll just be giving you a little something to take the edge off."

Dr. Cook came in to see if everything was ready. It was. "What kind of music do you like?" he asked.

I thought quickly and rather flippantly said, "Brazilian jazz." It actually was true; I am particularly keen on a style of music called Bossa Nova. I find it relaxing.

"Well!" said Dr. Cook. "I don't think we've ever had that request before. We'll see what we can do." Apparently the team likes to play music during the procedure and the patients gets to select the genre.

Kelley had already gone to the cath lab so, after saying goodbye to Charlie, I was wheeled by Melissa through the hallways and into the lab. It was a large room with a prominent table in the middle, a device over the top that looked like a camera, and large TV screens on the wall. There was a glassed-in control booth where Kelley was busy with something but she greeted me as Melissa wheeled me in. I scooted from the gurney to the operating table and then things started happening.

Melissa was over my right shoulder and Kelley announced she'd found some Brazilian jazz. The music started playing quietly — I believe it was *Corcovado* by Antônio Carlos Jobim — and Dr. Cook came in. My right arm was securely strapped down — this is where the catheter would be inserted — and my body was draped with a plastic cloth. "To minimum the risk of infection," I was told.

There were several other people in the room and they introduced themselves to me, then Kelley called a "time out." She announced to the room, "This is Mr. Martin Ramsay, date of birth May 3, 1956, here for a heart catheterization procedure." She went on to give several details about the procedure. "Are we all agreed?"

One by one, everyone in the room, including Dr. Cook, had to give a verbal agreement that that was what they were there for. They didn't ask me — I suppose the patient is already committed — but I was impressed that nothing was going to move forward until everyone was in agreement and on the same page.

With that, Dr. Cook instructed Melissa to give me 50 ccs of something, I assume it was the anesthesia, and Melissa repeated that back to him. I can't say that the drug made an obvious difference to me as I was still fully conscious, but, in hind sight, I did seem to be rather relaxed about the whole affair.

Dr. Cook told me he would numb my wrist where the cath would go in and suggested that, when he injected the lidocaine, it might be the most painful thing about the whole procedure. It wasn't bad; the three sticks to get the IV started were worse. He kept me informed about the entire procedure: when the initial opening was made into my radial artery, that he was going to inject a medication to relax the artery, when the catheter was first being inserted. "You'll probably feel the medication traveling up your arm," he said, and indeed I did. It was a warming, slightly burning sensation that traveled up my arm and then dissipated above the elbow. Then I realized the procedure was beginning because, on the TV screen on the wall, I could see the shadow of a beating heart and a wire inching closer and closer.

Of course I realized this was not some abstract image of a heart, this was my heart, the only one I had. I was torn between wanting to look away because it seemed so dramatic, so intimate, and wanting to watch because it was fascinating. Mostly I watched.

Occasionally there would be a little puff of what looked like smoke come out of the end of the catheter. I later realized this was the dye being injected into my aorta. Dr. Cook and the woman to his right, who appeared to be the operator of the X-ray camera, kept a murmured dialogue as Dr. Cook piloted the catheter here and there and the camera operator adjusted the location and angle of the camera so that they could get a good image of what they were seeing.

In hindsight, I realize the camera was not really a camera, but an X-ray generator and that the sensor must have been underneath me, integral to the table. The effect, however, was a live image of the three dimensional configuration that was me and my heart showing up as sharp shadows when Dr. Cook found the entrance to a coronary artery and was able to inject dye into the vessel. Soon what were clearly arteries were displaying on the TV screen.

Of course the details of what they were seeing had little meaning for me as my knowledge of coronary anatomy was limited to what I'd learned in high school biology. I now wish I'd studied up a bit more; it would have made the procedure more meaningful.

After what seemed like a very short time, perhaps 30 to 40 minutes, Dr. Cook announced he was done and would be removing the catheter. A band was placed around my wrist that had an inflatable pillow to put serious pressure on the opening. Apparently a major concern is bleeding from the artery, so the entire team was focused on making sure the wound was closed and sealed.

Dr. Cook then got my attention. "I'm afraid we couldn't put in a stent," he said. I was disappointed. I thought that was the whole purpose of this procedure. "The location of the blockage isn't a place I could do a stent." He also said something about me having an "anomalous configuration" — whatever that meant.

Dr. Cook left and, one by one, the other members of the team finished up their work. I was aware enough to thank them each for the role they had played and how much I appreciated their skill. Soon Melissa and Kelley were wheeling me back to the room where Charlie was waiting.

"Did Dr. Cook come in and talk to you?" Kelley asked Charlie.

"Yes," she said.

I have to confess that I was still fairly ignorant of what was going on. The only thing that had sunk into my brain was that the stent didn't get to happen. Beyond that, I just understood that I had some kind of blockage. Next steps hadn't occurred to me yet.

Melissa became concerned about the pressure band on my wrist. She felt like there was some swelling above the band, so she called over the heart cath lab and asked if they could bring a second pressure band.

When the young woman arrived — I believe she was the one operating the X-ray equipment — I asked her what she thought about what she had seen.

She looked at me intently and said, "I thought, 'Oh, that's not good!'" That was my first inkling that perhaps there was something quite serious going on.

Dr. Cook returned. "So ... this is serious?" I asked.

He looked at me as if I hadn't been paying attention before. I suppose I really wasn't. "Yes," he said. "This is very serious. You have a blockage just in front of a place where your arteries branch out into three. A trifurcation." Apparently this was one of the ways my heart was unusual; most people have two, a bifurcation. "I can't put a stent in there, right where the arteries branch off. You're going to need bypass surgery. We need to route blood around the blockage to each of the three arteries. In addition, you have two blockages in two branches of your circumflex artery. Those aren't as serious, but they're still a problem. I had a hard time finding those because the route those arteries take around the back of your heart is also anomalous." Apparently I'm just a special person with anomalies all over the place.

"You're saying this is a big deal?"

"Yes." Dr. Cook was very serious. "This is a big deal. You need surgery and you need it soon. I'm going to get you in to see a surgeon, preferably this week." It was a Wednesday. That meant he was sending me to a surgeon within the next two days.

My world was beginning to turn upside down.

Dr. Cook explained, at least as much as I was able to take in, that bypass surgery is serious. My breastbone, the sternum, would need to be sawn in half lengthwise. My chest would need to be opened up and my ribs pried back to give access to my heart. The surgeon would then need to add some blood vessels that routed blood around the blockage — bypasses. "I think you'll need at least five bypasses, possibly even six," said Dr. Cook. "The recovery is long. You'll need to be off work at least a month, preferably two. You'll need to sleep on your back so that your sternum can heal. That takes a while and you don't want to put any pressure or twisting on the bone while it knits back together." I was really beginning to understand that my routine — work, sleep, everything — was going to be completely disrupted.

Charlie and I looked at each other. We've always been there for each other. I knew she'd be there for me, but this really bothered me. It sounded like I wouldn't be able to there for her. I'd be almost an invalid. My mind was staggering as I tried to process this.

Dr. Cook gave us a list of three surgeons he recommended, one at the University of Kentucky Medical Center, one at Central Baptist Hospital, and one a Saint Joseph Hospital East. Of course none of the doctors' names was familiar. I wasn't keen on UK Med Center since it was a teaching hospital and I felt like, if I was going to have my chest opened up, I would rather have that done by an expert who knew what he or she was doing. We had friends who had good experience at Central Baptist, but, in the end we selected my surgeon using a simplistic criterion: Saint Joe East was the easiest to get to and had the best parking. I knew Charlie would have to drive the 40 miles from Berea while I was in the hospital, so I wanted the facility to be easy to get to since she prefers not to drive in city traffic.

"OK," said Dr. Cook. "Let me see what I can arrange with Dr. Dimeling."

Melissa and Kelley continued to monitor my wrist for bleeding and swelling. They were very attentive, reducing the pressure on the bands a tiny bit every 15 minutes. This turned out to be the longest part of the procedure.

Apparently that is typical for a heart cath; monitoring the catheterization site for bleeding takes much more time than the actual procedure itself.

Dr. Cook came back and said that he wasn't able to get an appointment with Dr. Dimeling this week, so I was to report to him first thing Monday morning to discuss the surgery I needed. "In the mean time," he said, "Take it easy. I'd say don't lift anything over 10 pounds — about the weight of a gallon of milk." That in itself scared me. Was I that in danger of something bad happening?

Charlie asked him, "Is this what they call the 'widow-maker'?"

Dr. Cook locked eyes with her. "I don't like using that term," he said, rather sternly I thought. "But I can't stress enough that this blockage is in a bad place." We thanked him, still trying to process this massive change that was barreling down on us.

Melissa and Kelley were so attentive and kind, helping to answer more questions as they occurred to us. After about two hours, I was ready to go home.

When we got in the car, Charlie drove and I started looking up where Dr. Dimeling's office was. It wasn't at Saint Joe East, it was at Saint Joe Main, the big hospital downtown rather than the one that was easy to get to on Richmond Road. I'm sorry to say this was the first of two times that I really lost it. I felt we had been mislead — there is a big difference between Saint Joe East and Saint Joe Main. Had I known that I would have selected Central Baptist instead. We called our daughter-in-law, Clarissa, who had worked as an RN at Saint Joe Main before she and Mark were married. What did she know about cardiac surgeons at Saint Joe? Had she ever heard of Dr. George Dimeling? Who would she recommend as a heart surgeon?

I also called Kelly in Dr. Cook's office asking if we couldn't get the doctor changed. I was frustrated, inappropriately so, and I fear I was short with Kelly. Of course it wasn't her fault. I think, in hind site, the magnitude of what I was facing made me subconsciously want to try to control something. If I couldn't control the need for major surgery, at least I could try to control which hospital my wife would have to drive to and find parking. Realistically, though, the wheels were already in motion and changing surgeons now would be difficult.

We Googled Dr. Dimeling and discovered that he had trained at Stanford and had most recently been on staff at Cleveland Clinic, but had moved to Lexington because his wife was from the area. Apparently family was important to him, yet we had a surgeon with impeccable credentials. That seemed positive.

We began to accept that Dr. George Dimeling would be my surgeon and that I would be going to Saint Joe Main.

Jolt

The next few days were difficult. I didn't know anything, yet I knew that I had to go through something enormous. I didn't know when it would happen, but I knew that it would likely be soon and then I'd have to plan on a lengthy recovery. This wasn't going to be a quick out-patient procedure. And then there was that looming concern: my heart was going to be messed with in a major way. Would I even survive?

My mind was in turmoil. Charlie was wonderful; we really treasured the time we had during those days. I also turned to the Bible for comfort.

The first verse that came to me was John 11:25 in which Jesus said, "I am the resurrection, and the life: he that believeth in me, though he were dead, yet shall he live." That helped. Even if I didn't make it through the surgery, I would still live eternally. There was nothing to fear, only the pain of separation from those I loved and only for a time.

I had to ask myself a difficult question: Was I ready to die? After several days of soul searching, it was settled. Yes, I was ready to go. I reflected on my life and, while I had been woefully inadequate in many ways, I knew in Whom I had placed my trust. I also knew that I had made the most of the time I had, investing in my grandchildren, children, wife and friends. I had worked to provide accurate and useful teaching in my Sunday School class. I had tried to have the utmost integrity in my business dealings. None of those things were adequate; only Jesus was sufficient, and I'd placed my faith in Him. But still, I was pleased to look back over my life and know that I could die without regrets. Yes, I was ready to go.

Once that question was settled, another verse came to me. I had taught 1 and 2 Thessalonians just a few months ago and a verse I'd been mulling over suddenly pushed its way to the foreground: 1 Thessalonians 5:19. It is a simple verse, but packed with implications: "Quench not the Spirit."

The Bible teaches that, once we become a follower of Jesus Christ, the Holy Spirit takes up residence inside us. (See Ephesians 1:14.) Further, 1 Corinthians 6:19-20 tells us, "Do you not know that your bodies are temples of the Holy Spirit, who is in you, whom you have received from God? You are not your own; you were bought at a price. Therefore honor God with your bodies." It seemed to me that, because of these blockages I had, the Holy Spirit needed to do a bit of renovation in His temple.

It was clear to me that, whatever might happen in all of this, I was to allow the Spirit of God which was in me to shine through. That meant I didn't need to indulge in self-pity or whining. I didn't need to spend time asking "why me?" I needed to face this and prepare for it, as best I could, and let others know where my strength and my sense of peace came from. Despite this jolt I had received, I resolved to do everything I could so that God's work in this would be obvious.

I also reflected on something else: the places where this blockage could have gone undetected were many. Dr. Devers could have brushed off my comment about being short of breath in Yellowstone, figuring I was indeed, getting older and out of shape. Instead he took it seriously enough to recommend a stress test. During the stress test, I could have quit once I'd reached the goal heart rate of 131 beats per minute. Instead I kept going. I wasn't sure, but it seemed that, had I not done that, the s-t wave depression that Dr. Cook spotted might have gone undetected. And Dr. Cook was willing to treat my problem with medication, but gently urged me to do the heart cath. Even more miraculous, I was willing to have the procedure done.

It seemed clear to me that God was orchestrating events so that I would end up having bypass surgery. The reasons He would do that were unclear to me, but I knew that they were important. I continued to pray and to seek God's guidance on why He had placed me in this situation.

On Sunday we went to church as usual and I taught my Sunday School class. At the end, I reserved a bit of time to explain what was happening.

"It looks like I'm going to need major surgery, folks." I proceeded to explain about the blockage that had been found, even drawing a rough diagram on the white board. "I don't know when the surgery will be done, but I'll probably find out tomorrow when Charlie and I visit the surgeon. The bad news is that I'm likely going to have to stop teaching Sunday School for a month, maybe two. Fortunately Todd is going to be able to take over."

Todd Wilson was my able backup. Usually that meant filling in a Sunday here or there when I was traveling for work or, in the case of our trip out west, ostensibly on vacation. But this was much more serious. Todd had a job and a young family himself, so I really appreciated his willingness to step up and teach the class. "I'll let you know just as soon as the surgeon gives me an idea of when he'll do the operation," I said.

People in the class were concerned, of course. We had become quite close over the years and I often referred to them as my "other family." They committed to praying for me and I promised to keep them informed.

We went home to host lunch for the usual crowd of 21 kids and grandkids.

After lunch, I asked Charlie and the three boys to come down to my office in the basement. I knew it was woefully inadequate, but I thought I could at least point them in the right direction should I become incapacitated, or worse. I showed them the various computers and what each one did. I explained how to receive in a check from a client since several were expected in the next week or so. And I showed them the three-ring binder I tried to keep up to date that contained documentation about systems, the network configuration, passwords, and much more.

The boys tried to take it in; I knew I was asking them to drink out of a fire hose. I also knew that the bulk of the burden was likely to fall on John Paul since he worked in technology and would most likely be able to spot what might need to be done should there be a problem.

It was a sobering time. I was not ready to hand my business off to others because there was too much in my head not committed to paper. Yet I might be forced to do just that, depending on the timing of the surgery, what happened during the surgery, and the speed with which I was able to recover.

I started trying to think in those terms.

Surgeon

Monday morning, quite early, we headed for Lexington. Charlie drove, saying, "I need the practice so I can find St. Joe hospital again."

Dr. Dimeling's office was in one of the medical annex buildings across Harrodsburg Road from the main hospital. It was the first day of August.

We did the usual paperwork — "May I see your ID and insurance card? Do you have any COVID symptoms? Do you want us to be able to talk to your wife about your medical conditions? Can you sign here proving we've told you about our HIPPA privacy policy?" Then we were ushered into a room. A nice lady took my vital signs and asked a few more questions. A bit later, we met Dr. Dimeling.

Dr. George Dimeling was rather young (*a good thing*, I thought, *not so young as to be untested but young enough to be energetic and up on the best techniques*). He looked at me and said, "I guess you've been having a lot of symptoms, right?"

"No, not at all," I told him. I explained about the Yellowstone event. "Other than that, I feel fairly good. I've always seemed to be relatively healthy."

"That's good," he said. "Because your blockages are in some bad places. You really do need surgery and you need it soon. The good news is that we know what the problem is and that we can fix it. This is not like a cancer diagnosis where we can hope we can solve the problem, but we can't be sure. I do a lot of bypass surgeries like this; you'll feel like a new man once you get through the recovery."

He explained that he planned on doing six bypass grafts to supply blood to my heart beyond the blockages. "I'll use arteries as much as I can," he said. "They seem to work better. But I won't be able to do all the bypasses that way. We'll also need to take a vein out of your leg and use that for some of them. I have a game plan in my mind about what I'll do, but every situation can be a little different. If I need to adjust the plan, I will, once I get inside."

We had a frank conversation about how serious this surgery would be. "The problem really isn't going to be your heart," Dr. Dimeling said. "When I finish with the bypass grafts, your heart will be fixed. You'll have some very fancy plumbing, but it will be fixed. The problem is that I have to go through your sternum to do get inside your chest, and bones take a long time to heal. I will wire your breast bones back together, but you will need to be really careful with it so that it can heal straight and properly. I don't want you lifting more than five pounds. I don't want you driving. I want you to sleep on your back, not on your side or stomach as that would put torque on your sternum. A lot of people find it is easier to sleep in a recliner than in a bed. It's going to be a long haul; you should plan on being off work for at least eight weeks."

My world had already been turned upside down, but this was confirming the inversion.

"Will you … will you stop my heart?" I asked. I wondered: even if I come through this, will there be a time when I am clinically dead?

"Many surgeons do, but I don't. I would rather keep your heart beating so that we don't have to start it again. You can get blood clots that way, and we want to avoid that."

"You mean you're able to sew blood vessels onto a beating heart?"

I think I caught a touch of modesty. He simply said, "Yes."

I didn't ask about breathing, partly because I really didn't want to know and partly because I already knew — I would not be breathing on my own. A ventilator would be doing the breathing for me. I was going to be completely at the mercy of the technology and, more to the point, of the skill of the team doing the operation. My first trust was in the Lord that His will would be done. My second trust was in Dr. Dimeling and his team, people I hadn't even met yet.

Dr. Dimeling explained more about the procedure. I fear I didn't take it all in, but I gathered there would be some kind of port in my subclavian artery that would be used to reroute my blood through a machine that would oxygenate it during the surgery. That port would also be used to deliver the anesthesia and other drugs that might be required. There would be another port in my wrist that was used to monitor blood pressure and other key vitals constantly. Even the Foley catheter that was used to take urine away from my body would have a sensor in it to track my body temperature. It sounded like there would be an awful lot of tubes connected to my body.

The surgery itself would take five to six hours. *That's a long time to be opened up*, I thought to myself. *And poor Charlie. I'll be out of it, but she'll be on pins and needles waiting to hear how things are going.* After surgery I would go directly to the cardiac care unit; no recovery room as I would be recovering in the CCU. I would spend at least one day in the CCU, possibly more if there were complications. Then I would be sent to a regular hospital room, where I would probably be discharged after three more days. All told, I would probably be in the hospital for five days before I went home to begin the long, arduous recovery.

If I could have looked at myself from the outside, there would have been two of me. One part of me was trying desperately to process all of this that was going to be happening and reeling from the shock of how my life was changing. The other part of me, I would even say the larger part of me, was thinking, *well, if this is what has to happen, let's make it work the best we possibly can. I wouldn't have chosen this for myself but, since it is happening, with God's help, I can do this.* I also was very grateful for a wife who was with me all the way.

"Dr. Dimeling," I asked. "Have I brought this on myself? Was it riotous living — too little exercise and poor diet — that caused this blockage?"

His look was sincere. "I don't think we can blame this one on lifestyle," he said. "We have to chalk it up to genetics."

So, had we not caught this, I would have been one of those men who suddenly dropped dead of a heart attack.

Charlie asked, "So, if Martin did have a heart attack ..."

"He would not survive an 'event'," said Dr. Dimeling with finality. "He needs this surgery and he needs it soon. Unless you have any more questions, I'm going to go get my scheduling people working on finding a time when we can do the surgery. We don't want to wait any longer than we have to."

Dr. Dimeling left us and we sat in his examining room, talking over what we had heard. Looking back, we were surprisingly upbeat. We knew it was serious and we knew that we needed to move quickly. We knew that there were major risks of having the surgery, but were also convinced that there were even greater risks if I didn't have the surgery. I was so grateful to Charlie; her support was essential. We were beginning to solidify our attitude and our approach. The verse from 1 Thessalonians came to me again: quench not the Spirit.

We waited for almost an hour before Dr. Dimeling returned with the lady who did the surgery scheduling. In hindsight, I realize that they were doing a lot of work, moving schedules around, calling in favors to get the operating room booked, working out the details.

I was to return to the hospital on Wednesday, just two days from now, at 7:30 AM, to get all my pre-op registration and testing done. I would need to fill out a lot of paperwork, have an ultrasound of my wrist and carotid artery to ensure I had sufficient blood flow, do some complex lung function tests to make sure I could tolerate the ventilator, and have a pre-op exam. "Your appointment with pre-op is for 11:00 AM," the scheduling lady said. "All told, plan for the entire process to take four to five hours. The day of the surgery will be Friday, August 5. You'll report to the pre-op area at 6:30 AM, but you won't need to register because that will all be taken care of on Wednesday."

So, in case you're counting, that meant that, four days from now, I'd be in surgery and out of action for a week in the hospital and then two months at home. That wasn't much time to prepare, and it again underscored the sense of urgency that the medical professionals were feeling about getting me into surgery.

"Go home and take it very, very easy," said Dr. Dimeling.

"Easy, as in …?"

"Don't lift anything over five pounds." *A jug of milk weighs more than that*, I thought. "Just rest. Try to reduce stress …"

Easy for you to say, Doc. I'm about to have my chest flayed open like a fish! "My cousin and I go walking about three miles in the morning …?"

Again, that sincere look. "Stop doing that," said the doctor.

I was getting the message.

We had one more stop to make before we finished with Dr. Dimeling's office. We were asked to go see Debbie at the end of the hallway.

Debbie introduced herself as the "nurse navigator" who would be watching my case. "I'm an RN," she explained, "and my job is to be your advocate and help you navigate through the complex thing that is going to happen to you. I have all kinds of tools I can use to follow your case. And I'm going to give you my personal number so you can call me at any time if you have questions." She was a smart lady. She handed the number to Charlie.

She again walked us through what the recovery would be like. Debbie was very likable and easy to talk to. We were able to ask more questions and receive reassuring responses.

During the conversation it came out that I would need to find someone to teach my Sunday School class during my recovery. She asked more about that and we discovered that all three of us shared a faith in Jesus Christ. That made the conversation even better. I fear there were several times I got a bit choked up as I said that I truly was ready to go but that, if I survived this, God clearly seemed to have some mission for me. He was intervening in this dramatic way for some purpose as yet unseen and unknown.

The more we chatted the more we liked each other. I suppose it was during our recounting of the Yellowstone episode that led to the blockage being discovered that we got to talking about rivers. On our western trip we had gone north through Minnesota (one of the five states we were missing) and I had gotten to see the headwaters of the Mississippi, where it is a little creek. We had also followed, to some degree, the path of the Lewis and Clark expedition on the Missouri River. That led to a debate: which was longer, the Mississippi or the Missouri? I said I thought I'd heard it was the Missouri even though that was counter-intuitive. Debbie was inclined to think it was the Mississippi. I told her that she had a homework assignment. Assuming I survived this surgery, when I came for my post-op visit several weeks from now, I expected her to have done the research and to have a definitive answer in the Mississippi vs. Missouri debate.

We parted on great terms and Charlie and I went to P. F. Chang's Chinese restaurant for a very late lunch and to continue to talk over what was about to happen.

Preparation

I was in panic mode. I had three days, really only two since we would have to be in Lexington for the pre-op work on Wednesday, until the surgery on Friday. Since, assuming I came through the surgery OK, I wouldn't be able to do much of anything for the next two months, my planning had to include a fairly large block of time. Clearly I wasn't going to be able to do any kind of detailed preparation. I was going to have to triage what needed to be done and only do the most urgent things.

While I never sat down and made a detailed list, I knew there were many things I was going to have to let go. Those included:
- Answering email, text messages and the telephone
- Running the business, both CEATH Company and the LAMP Consortium
- Teaching my Sunday School class
- Gardening, including weeding, harvesting, and so on
- Tending to the goats, including daily feeding
- Filling the woodshed to prepare for the coming winter
- Basic household maintenance that Charlie counted on from me

I would have to rely on others to take care of these things and a thousand more while I recovered. I perceived that job one for me would be recovering. I would just have to let all of those things go, no easy task for someone who has been used to doing most everything for himself.

The first order of business was to take care of CEATH Company and the LAMP Consortium. After all, this was our only source of income. If that fell apart, we'd be in financial trouble. While I was beginning to think about retirement, I hadn't planned on scaling back my involvement with the company for years yet.

I did a rather detailed financial analysis. While it was not sustainable to hire Jeremy full time, finances were such that it could be managed for a year or more while paying both Jeremy and myself about the same amount. I called Jeremy and told him I'd like to make him a job offer.

It worked out well. Jeremy wanted to discuss it with his brother- and sister-in-law at the hardware store but, in the end, they were happy to let Jeremy pursue something he really enjoyed. Ultimately, Jeremy said he'd be happy to work for the LAMP Consortium full time.

Jeremy had proven himself to be invaluable in the business. He was even better than me at staying in touch with clients and keeping people happy. There were some technical aspects that he wasn't prepared to handle, but I hoped those would be few and far between. Perhaps by the time any issues arose, I might be enough recovered to deal with something. In the mean time, I finished up a few small projects I had been working on and updated the three ring binder I kept that contained all kinds of information about the company network, servers, accounts, and more. I knew John Paul would probably have to be Jeremy's technology backup if it came down to it. While I would have liked to have prepared both him and Jeremy better, there wasn't time. I was finding I had to trust that it would all work out.

I also began calling key clients to let them know what was happening. Those calls were tough. I was going from being the able consultant and entrepreneur they counted on, to being completely out of the picture. I tried to explain, as best I could, that this was completely unexpected, that it wasn't what I would choose, but that I was counting on them to understand and to give Jeremy all the grace and support they could during my recovery.

Many said they would be praying for me during the surgery and for my speedy recovery. Most asked to be kept informed. I knew I would not be in any shape to make lots of phone calls, so I would need to rely on Charlie and my sons to get the word out about how I was doing, regardless of what happened.

My colleague Nick in Toronto said something I thought was quite profound. He opined this surgery I was going to have was "almost miraculous, almost routine." He was right. The technology and the medical skill that was going to fix my problem was amazing. And yet, it has become commonplace enough that it was "almost routine."

I could tell, some of my clients got quite choked up over the phone. They recognized the seriousness of what I would be going through. Two of them took the time to pray at length with me over the phone. Those were quite emotional for me; no one was under any illusions about the many ways this could go badly. One got alarmed that Jeremy might not know how to do the creative projects I'd done for him in the past. I assured him that Jeremy knew how to do the routine things and that, if he had something really exotic, it would just have to wait until I could get back to work. I didn't know what else to say. There was only so much preparation I could do, given the short time I had.

Jeremy and I worked on an "away" message for my email so that, should someone send me a message, they would get an automated response saying that I was having to take some time off and that, in the meantime, Jeremy would be the primary contact person. We decided against saying why I was away; alarming just anyone who might casually email me that I was having open heart surgery might have been counter productive. Jeremy later told me that he had to call several clients and calm them down. They had assumed I had taken a sudden and capricious vacation and were a bit put out by my irresponsibility.

Jeremy explained, on a case by case basis, the actual nature of my absence and was able to reassure every one of them.

Dealing with my Sunday School class meant a call to Todd. "I know you said you'd be willing to be my backup," said, "but it is happening faster than I anticipated. Can you start this coming Sunday? I'll be in the cardiac care unit and in no shape to teach." Todd was wonderfully supportive.

I even went so far as to queue up two months worth of paychecks for Charlie and for Jeremy. I figured if I didn't make it through the surgery, I'd be giving them through the end of September to figure out what to do if I was no longer with them.

I had been scheduled for my regular hair cut on Wednesday. We thought it would be a good idea for me to get a trim before I went in for surgery. Who knew how long it would be before I had recovered enough to get my hair cut again? Obviously I couldn't go on Wednesday as I would be in Lexington doing all the pre-op work.

Charlie called Nancy, the lady who cuts my hair, and Nancy was able to move her schedule around to fit me in on Tuesday. "Cut it short," I said. "It may be a while before I can come back and get my hair cut again."

In a fit of optimism, we scheduled another appointment five weeks out. I was praying that, by then, I'd be able to return to Nancy for another haircut.

On Wednesday, August 3, we left home at 6:30 AM for the drive to Saint Joseph Hospital in Lexington. Charlie drove again so she could practice the route. We reported to the registration department. Very soon we were called back to an office and offered a chair by Elizabeth, the person who would be doing the registration.

I was trying to calm my nerves; this is not the kind of situation in which I excel. Filling out lots of paperwork in what seems like an incredibly bureaucratic system makes me a little crazy. Part of that, I'm sure, is because process consultation is what I had spent a lot of my life doing. I had helped many organizations improve their processes; in my experience healthcare is an industry that has some of the biggest problems. Part of my craziness, too, if I'm honest, is because I don't like being told what to do. I can hear Charlie saying, "Amen!" to that. If anything, it only serves to point out how flawed and selfish I am, deep down inside.

Elizabeth, fortunately, knew her job well and was also personable and friendly, even at this early hour. I gave Elizabeth my driver's license — to prove I was really who I said I was — and my insurance cards.

When I had turned 65 a little over a year ago, I had, of course, signed up for Medicare. It is a ritual, a rite of passage, all Americans apparently have to go though. Fortunately our insurance advisor, Mike Sills, had steered us into purchasing a Medicare supplement plan that covered what Medicare didn't cover.

This was the first time it dawned on me that this whole process was likely to be staggeringly expensive. I had no idea how much it would cost, and a part of me didn't want to know. I just knew, and was trusting, that the Medicare supplement plan I had been paying for would cover the remainder after Medicare had covered 80%. Even if I ended up being responsible for 20% of the cost of all of this, 20% of a very large number is still a lot of money.

At the same time that I might be owing a lot of money to the hospital and the doctors, I wouldn't be able to work and earn a living. I simply had to set worries about money aside.

Elizabeth asked lots of questions about my doctors, the procedure, my family medical history, the medications I was on, and much more. She recorded everything in her computer as we went along. Several times I had to sign something. I usually try to read what I'm being asked to sign — to me, signing something you haven't read is asking for trouble. Elizabeth was patient with me while I scanned the documents, but eventually I gave up and just signed where requested. I was beginning to get a sense of inevitability about all of this. Large wheels had already been set in motion that I seemed powerless to stop.

I suppose if I was going to decline to have the surgery, this was the time. Otherwise, I was making the final choice to proceed. My on-going conversation with the Lord had left me satisfied that doing the surgery was what He desired. It seemed that He had orchestrated so many details leading up to this moment that this was clearly His will. If He did not want me to have the surgery, He could have interrupted the process at many different points. While I was aware that the doctors could not predict that I would drop dead of an "event" as Dr. Dimeling called it — a heart attack — in the coming year, that seemed to be the consensus. Since I had this opportunity, it seemed clear that God was ordaining that Charlie not be deprived of her husband any time soon and that my family would continue to have their Dad and grandfather for some time yet.

Elizabeth also helped us understand about the hospital's visitation policy. Charlie would stay in the surgery waiting room during the five or more hours I was in the operating theater. From there I would be taken directly to the Cardiac Care Unit or CCU. Effectively, CCU is the recovery area for post open heart surgeries. Charlie would be allowed to see me briefly, but I would probably still be so anesthetized that it was unlikely I would be able to respond or remember it. She would then have to go home and could not return until 8:00 AM the following morning. She could stay with me in CCU until 5:00 PM, when she would have to go home again. However, most likely I would be sent to a regular room by the end of the day, where she would be allowed to stay. We struggled to figure out the best way to minimize Charlie's trips up and down the interstate and give me the support I might need after surgery.

I continued to answer Elizabeth's questions, sign documents, and (hopefully) participate with a cheerful attitude. It took about an hour, but we were finally finished. Elizabeth took us back to the waiting room, telling us that the people from ultrasound and respiratory would be along to do the pre-op testing that was needed.

The ultrasound tech was already there and ready to take me down the corridor.

I have made it a habit, as much as I could, to learn people's names and call them by that name. I know that I learned the ultrasound tech's name, but I can no longer recall what it was. As I write this, I've learned there really is such a thing as post-surgical brain fog. Her name has escaped through the sieve I call my brain. I know that we had a nice conversation and that she was very pleasant; I just can't recall the details I would like.

The purpose of the ultrasound was two-fold. First, the technician examined the arteries in my wrist. As I understood it, the purpose was to ensure that my arteries were healthy enough to support the all-important blood pressure monitoring equipment that would be used during surgery.

The second examination was of the carotid arteries in my neck. If I understood this procedure, she was making sure there was sufficient blood flow to my brain so that, during the stress of the surgery, there would not be the potential for deprivation of blood flow and oxygen. I joked and told her she'd better make sure because my brain was already compromised and I needed every little grey cell I could keep.

The ultrasound didn't take more than a half an hour. When it was done, I was taken back to the reception area where the respiratory therapist was waiting for me for her procedure.

This lady, whose name I've also lost, was a delightful, more mature woman. We had a lot in common despite our skin color being markedly different. She was getting close to retirement and was thinking about what she would do after she didn't have to come to work every day. That was a challenge I could resonate with; I was having similar considerations although mine was being brought on by this annoying little heart blockage rather than a voluntary consideration of my age. More important, she was a dedicated church-going woman and several members of her family were preachers or Sunday School teachers. We had a wonderful time talking as she prepared me for the lung function studies she needed to perform.

First I was given a breathing tube that was hooked to some sophisticated measuring equipment. My nose was clamped with what looked like a giant, high-tech clothes pin. My job was to draw as much air into my lungs as possible and then, on a signal from her, blow it all out into the tube as quickly as possible. I failed the first time — I didn't understand how serious she was about blowing it all out immediately and completely. "Let's try it again," she said, staring at her computer screen and clearly not satisfied with the result.

We did it three more times. She wanted to get an average measurement and wanted to discount the first failed attempt. Apparently I am full of hot air and this spirometry test demonstrated my lung capacity was adequate for the surgery during which I would need to be attached to a ventilator.

The second test was even more interesting. My friend had a tank of a helium-oxygen mix that was, as she explained, very precisely controlled so that the ratio of He to O_2 was known. The idea was that I would breathe in lungfuls of this mixture, hold it in my lungs for a set period of time and then, on a signal from my friend, expel it through the tube. The interesting thing to me as a chemistry major was that a sensor would then measure the ratio of helium to oxygen remaining after the gas had been in my lungs for a time. I gathered that this was to measure the rate of diffusion in my lungs. The gas would be picked up by the capillaries in my alveoli (the tiny sacs in the lungs where the magic exchange of life-giving O_2 for waste CO_2 happens) and, by measuring the ratio of helium to other gasses coming out of my lungs, the doctor would get an important measurement of my lungs' ability to oxygenate my blood.

Apparently I passed this test, too. I hoped all of the people who worked with me would be as charming as my new respiratory therapy friend.

❦

After the two sets of lab tests, we were told to go up to the pre-op area on the second floor to wait for the official pre-surgery registration. We were the only ones there so we reported to the receptionist and sat down to wait. I hoped that we wouldn't be waiting long since, by now, I was getting rather hungry.

In hind sight, I wish I had understood how seriously people took our "appointment" for pre-op as explained to us by the scheduling person in Dr. Dimeling's office two days earlier. She had, indeed, told us that our appointment was at 11:00. We had arrived in pre-op around 9:30 because of how efficient the ultrasound and respiratory testing had been. Charlie and I were both beginning to be concerned at the parade of people who arrived after us but who were taken ahead of us. I assumed what we would be taken in the order that we arrived. Not so. Apparently that appointment time was sacrosanct. Even so, it was about 11:15 when we were finally called.

This is a cautionary tale to myself. I allowed this scheduling disconnect to affect me. I shouldn't have. When we finally got back to the pre-op area, my attitude was not where it ought to have been. I was setting myself up for the second time I would behave badly during the ordeal.

We were shown into a rather cluttered area with 20 or more curtained booths. Each one apparently had surgery patients being prepared. The scene was rather chaotic with people coming and going and calling to each other. I was asked to sit down by a nurse who began asking lots of questions. A second person approached me from the other side and simply began to draw blood out of my arm. She didn't introduce herself and didn't even really explain what she was doing. I felt like I was being treated like a number, not a human being.

My blood pressure was taken and it was rather high. I said, "Well, y'all aren't helping any." I wish I hadn't said that. Of course my blood pressure was up. Being prepared for surgery was a stressful situation. The nurses could have helped ease my mind, but they were under no obligation to do so.

I'm sure both ladies were overworked, but it was as if they were looking for something to respond to. "What do you mean?" one demanded.

"We waited for 90 minutes to be shown back, other people were taken ahead of us, I don't know what's going on ..." It was lame and I knew it, but I plunged ahead. I was letting my temper run away with me, I'm very ashamed to say.

Dear Charlie helped soothe things over. She knows her husband well; he does not do well in situations like this and so she applied her incredible Tennessee charm in chatting with the ladies as they did their job. I tried to get control of myself, but I wasn't completely successful.

A lady in a white coat approached us and introduced herself as Dr. Mihaela Cornea from anesthesia. She wanted to make sure I was a good candidate for the extreme sedation I would receive during the surgery.

She was a friendly woman with an Eastern European accent I couldn't place. I asked her where she was from and she wanted me to guess. I guessed the Czech Republic. "Close," she said. "I'm originally from Romania, but I've lived here for over 20 years. All of my children were born here." She wanted to know my story and why I was having surgery.

I explained about the trip out west and how I'd experienced shortness of breath in Yellowstone. "Well, thank goodness for Yellowstone!" she exclaimed.

She examined my mouth and tongue, asked about allergies, and made sure everything was a good as it could be.

She could tell I was nervous. She said something that really stuck and helped reassure me. "I understand," Dr. Cornea said, "that you're nervous about this. To you this is a big deal, and it is a big deal. But," she added, "you need to understand that, to us, this is routine. We do this kind of surgery every day. We know what we're doing and we'll take very good care of you."

After Dr. Cornea left I was given more instructions, including a device called an incentive spirometer and a packet of antibacterial pads I was to use to scrub my body in advance of the surgery. I was told to report back to pre-op at 6:00 AM on Friday for the surgery.

With that, we were finally free to go and get something to eat.

At home, I tried out the incentive spirometer. This was a hand-held plastic device with a breathing tube attached to it. There was a little ball in one chamber that lifted when I inhaled with my mouth around the tube. Breathe in too fast and the ball rose too high; breathe in too slowly and the ball didn't rise enough. The goal was to keep the ball in the middle. A second round chamber, like a piston cylinder, had a moveable disk of plastic that would rise up as I inhaled. The idea was to empty my lungs as much as possible, then place my lips around the tube and breathe in as deeply and as completely as possible. The little ball had to be kept between two marks while the piston disk rose up and up, indicating how much air I was able to get into my lungs.

The purpose of this little device was to force myself to fill my lungs, attempting to open up every little sack — the alveoli — as much as possible. Apparently the anesthesia and being on a ventilator tended to make the alveoli a bit sticky and one could lose lung capacity if one didn't get them back into action as soon as possible after surgery. There was also the very real danger of pneumonia setting in.

I practiced on the device to see how much capacity my lungs had prior to surgery. I wasn't clear if the metric was in milliliters, but I was able to inhale between 2,500 and 2,750 on the device.

The device is called an "incentive" spirometer because there is a little arrow that slides so that you can set it to your goal volume. I dutifully set the incentive level to 2,750.

Charlie felt that we needed to get a recliner that would lie flat that I could sleep in. Since I'm a side sleeper and sleeping on my back would be a requirement for two months, it seemed advisable to have a chair that wouldn't allow me to roll over in my sleep. It would also be advisable if the chair had an electric motor that would lie back and raise up, rather than having to use a handle for that purpose. We believed that a handle would require more than five pounds of strain.

We had developed a great relationship with a local store, Hays Furniture, and Charlie went to check out the inventory while I was taking care of more business details. She found two that she thought might do and had me come look. Patty Coyle, the proprietress, was eager to help in my rather urgent situation.

I liked one chair in particular. It fit my body well and was quite comfortable. I hoped I would be able to sleep in that recliner. "We'll take this one," we told Patty.

"I'll have it delivered this afternoon," she replied. That is what working with a local small business is like. They take a personal interest in their customers and take care of their needs.

The chair arrived as promised before I had to head to the hospital.

We made one final decision. Rather than having to set an alarm clock for 3:30 AM to get up, get showered and drive the hour plus to the hospital on Friday morning, Charlie thought it would be smart to get a hotel room at a hotel across the street from the hospital. She didn't want us to have to be worrying about possible traffic jams or car trouble. I agreed. While some people might have trouble sleeping in a hotel bed, I didn't have that problem. My job had required so much travel that I was fairly comfortable sleeping on the road.

Charlie called and, as it turned out, the hotel across the street from the hospital had a special rate for patients and their families. I suggested we get two nights so that, after my surgery was over, Charlie wouldn't have to drive back to Berea exhausted, only to turn around and come back the next day. We would stay together in the hotel room on Thursday night; Charlie would return to the room on Friday night after my surgery while I was recovering in CCU. She'd then be able to be in my room at 8:00 on Saturday morning.

Around 3:00 PM on Thursday, August 4, we headed to Lexington. I packed a backpack with a few things I thought I might like — a book to read, a pad of paper, my new incentive spirometer. I also brought those antibacterial pads I had been given. Charlie packed an overnight bag for two nights.

We tried to distract ourselves by going to the mall. Charlie shopped a bit, but I was too preoccupied to do much more than follow along. We had a nice dinner together and, despite the dramatic change that was about to overtake us, we both had a sense of calm that this was going to work out. Even if I didn't come through the surgery, we were both confident that this was the right thing to do. "God is completely in charge of this," Charlie reassured me. "I know," I replied. "I'm ready to go. My only regret will be not being there for you." I knew that, for a surgery this complicated, there were a thousand things that could go wrong. I just had to be OK with that.

As we were walking down through the mall to go to the hotel, we were surprised to meet some dear friends from Berea. Tim and Kay were in Lexington because Tim was also facing some major medical challenges. When Charlie told them why were were in Lexington, they were surprised, but Tim immediately said, "Let's pray."

Right there in the middle of the mall we joined hands in a circle and Tim prayed fervently and urgently for my protection, for the doctors and staff who would be doing the surgery, for Charlie's strength and courage, and that God's will would be done. It was an uplifting time; again I had the strong sense in my Spirit that God was in control.

Once we had checked into the hotel, we decided to walk around a bit. We found a little store and Charlie bought a few snacks to keep her company in the hotel the next night. She made the mistake of asking the clerk if this was a safe area. "Well," he replied, "I wouldn't exactly say that. It's OK during the daytime, but I wouldn't go around walking after dark. We just had a shooting a couple of blocks from here night before last." And with that cheery information we scuttled back to the hotel.

Before turning in for the night, I was to shower and use those antibacterial pads after showering. The instructions were very specific. There were six cloths; each was to be used on a specific area of my body. One was for arms, one for legs, one for the front of my chest, and so on. The instructions explained that the purpose of this was to minimize the bacteria on my skin that could inadvertently get inside my body during the surgery and cause an infection.

The pads were soaked with a slightly sticky substance that smelled, not unpleasant, but rather like a chemical factory. After applying them all over my body, I felt gooey and in need of another shower. Instead, we turned out the light and tried to sleep.

At 2:30 AM the alarm on my phone went off. I had set it because I had to get up again and do the antibacterial pad exercise a second time with a second set of pads. I can't say I was thrilled to be woken up to slime myself all over again, but I did it. I really did want to follow the medical advice as closely as possible so as to minimize any risks over which I might have some tenuous control.

All too early the alarm clock went off again. This time it was for real — I was heading to the hospital and major, major surgery.

Surgery

A hospital at 6:00 AM is an eerily different place. Entire offices are closed and dark. There are shadows in corners that, during the day, will be filled with people. No interns in scrubs are hurrying down the corridors. Nobody is standing in front of the elevator doors peering anxiously at the lighted floor numbers above. No patients are being transported in wheelchairs from here to there. No visitors are pretending to drink cups of bad coffee as they tensely wait for their loved one to come out of an important diagnostic test.

We had been given a "go directly to surgery" card during the pre-op routine on Wednesday that let us bypass admissions. There wasn't anyone in admissions anyway. Nor was there anyone at the surgery entrance, just a sign by the phone that said, "If the desk is unattended, call this number." We called. "I'll be there in a few minutes," we were told.

Charlie and I were escorted down the hallway to the same area where my pre-op workup had been done. But this time we were shown to a curtained alcove with a bed. It was show time.

I was given a gown and told to undress. Charlie took my clothes, my glasses, my wallet, my cell phone, and even my wedding ring. I wondered how many days it would be before I would get them back. I was mentally prepared to go cold turkey off of the cell phone. But the wedding ring? That was something I'd been wearing almost non-stop for 47 years. I had a lump in my throat as I took it off and handed it to my life partner.

Two nurses took charge of me, asking the same questions I'd been asked before, making sure I was the right patient for the right surgery. One was relatively new on the job; she had been hired because of her expertise on some software that St. Joseph was going to be transitioning to. The project had been delayed, she told me, so she was working in pre-op. It was kind of fun watching the two of them as the second nurse was experienced with the old, current software. Together they were getting my data entered but also using it as an opportunity to train the new nurse on the old system. Had I not been the patient and instead had been their consultant, I could have related to their struggles as I had helped many organizations through similar transitions.

The time for the thing I secretly dreaded most was upon us: they needed to get the IV started. I knew my veins would be hard to find because I couldn't help being nervous. But they got it in one, for which I was grateful. There were other indignities to go through, however. My chest and groin were shaved, the chest for obvious reasons, the groin because they might need to harvest a vein out of my leg to use for some of the bypasses.

Mark, Luke and John Paul had arrived. They were going to be there for their mother while I was in surgery which filled me with pride and gratitude. They knew what they needed to do and were acting on that knowledge.

They were allowed back two at a time once the final preparations were complete. Mark and Luke came first. I said goodbye to each one and told them how much I loved them. Mark said, "Dad, you really have no regrets, do you? You're really ready to go if the Lord calls you home."

"Yes," I said. "Totally ready. You boys know what I expect. Lead godly lives. Take care of your wives and your kids. Take care of Mom. I'll be fine."

John Paul came back with Greg, our pastor. It was good to see him and I appreciated that he had made the trip to Lexington so early in the morning given his brutal schedule. I told John Paul how proud I was of him and how much I loved him. Greg led us in prayer.

The anesthesiologist came in. It wasn't Dr. Cornea from two days ago; this was a man with an African accent. He said his name was Dr. Ghansa and he asked me the questions anesthesiologist need to ask: Had I ever had a reaction to anesthesia? No. Did I have any breathing difficulties? No. Did I have any concerns? Other than being put so deeply under that machines would be breathing for me, circulating my blood for me, and basically keeping me alive? No.

I asked him where he was from. I said I detected a West African accent and he smiled and said he was from Ghana. I told him I had a college chum years ago who was from Ghana and told him my friend's name. Dr. Ghansa said that, based on the surname, he knew where in Ghana my friend must have grown up.

Then it was just Charlie and me. There didn't seem to be much to say — we had already said what needed to be said. There was just the companionable, loving silence that only two people who know each other extremely well can share and be comfortable with.

Then the nurses announced it was time to go.

Charlie went with me down another hallway. At a turn in the corridor, the three boys were waiting. Apparently they had been told I'd be coming that way so I got to say goodbye one last time. One nurse had called this the "kissing corner" so Charlie gave me a quick peck, the automatic doors opened, and I was headed to the inner sanctum.

The operating room had a wall of glass facing the corridor. The operating table was prominent in the middle of the room with very large lights mounted overhead. Four or five people were already in the room. As I was wheeled past a large apparatus that had lots of glass tubes a woman introduced herself to me, saying, "I'll be your perfusionist today." It suddenly hit me that my blood would soon be flowing through those tubes, infusing it with oxygen and keeping it circulating while my heart was being worked on.

I was asked to slide onto the operating table which was cold and stainless steel and surprisingly narrow. I was asked if I could "scoot over about an inch more" which I managed to do.

Dr. Ghansa was there at my head. I couldn't see him, but the rich bass of his West African accent was unmistakable. "I see you're from Berea," he said. "I know someone from Berea."

"Oh really?" I replied. "Who is that?"

"His last name is Burberry."

"You mean Keith Burberry?"

"Yes!" Dr. Ghansa was amazed. "Do you know him?"

"Sure," I said. "I've known Keith from when he was a little kid," I said. "His father was the pastor of the Methodist Church."

Dr. Ghansa chuckled. "He's on vacation this week, but I'm going to have to text him about you. He's one of the partners in our anesthesiologist group." Several people who were working in the room chimed in, making comments about it being a small world. There seemed to be a good sense of camaraderie and teamwork in the room.

And that is about the last of my memories in the operating room. Someone must have slipped some medication in my IV because the next memories I have were from much later. In hindsight, I was very glad for that. Even before the surgery began in earnest, there were several things that had to be done, some of which I suspect might have been quite painful had I been awake.

I was in surgery for over five hours. Of course I knew nothing of this and only know about it from what Charlie told me afterwards. Apparently Dr. Dimeling did a very good job of informing her about my progress. And the boys stayed with her through the long ordeal.

After the surgery was finished and I was patched back together, Charlie and the boys were allowed to see me very briefly.

I should warn anyone who has a loved one that undergoes heart surgery that this must be one of the toughest parts of the process. When someone comes out of such a massive surgery, they look dreadful. Charlie is tough, but for her to say how bad I looked tells me a lot. Be prepared that your husband or wife or other family member will appear to have been through a terrible ordeal. I guess, after all, they have. Their breast bone has been literally sawn in half. Their ribs have been retracted to open up a gaping hole into their chest. People have had their hands in that cavity and have been working on the organ that we think of as the home of our emotions, of our very being. Machines have been breathing for them, oxygenating their blood and pumping it through their body.

I don't remember any of this, of course.

Luke said that he told me he loved me, to which I apparently cogently replied, "Mrff zygliulg shnarfnec foozlegurp."

Later I learned that the boys had taken care of making sure Charlie got something to eat and made sure she got safely back to the hotel to spend the night.

I spent the night in the Cardiac Care Unit in a blissful anesthetically-induced stupor. I remember my throat being very sore, undoubtedly from the ventilator. I vaguely remember a nurse, I believe her name was Justine, checking on me. I was dimly aware that there were tubes and wires all over me, along with beeps and hums and other equipment noises. But mostly I was out of it.

Unit

Toward morning (at least I assume it was morning) I began to be more aware of my surroundings. But my brain was still very much under the influence of the drugs I had been given. I had very vivid images and dreams that would swim across my conscience. I was very impressed with the creativity and importance of the ideas I was having and wished fervently that I could write them down so that I could recall and use them later.

Of course they were probably all nonsense.

I remember one pattern that was composed of broad arrows weaving in and out of each other, all with a color pallet of dark greens, olives, sages and emeralds. They were constantly moving, intersecting, forming patterns, then moving off in another direction. At the time I thought it was a stunning design and I recall thinking, "This is as good as anything M. C. Escher ever did."

Just goes to show you that drugs will mess with your mind.

Another image was an expansive field of brown, marked off into little squares. Some of the squares were flat, but some had been scored with an X so that the corners flapped back to reveal a fuzzy underside. It was almost as if this was a large sheet of some plant material that was ripening as indicated by the openings on the surface. Some of the openings contained a blue ball, like a blueberry. Others were empty, indicating the "fruit" (whatever it was) had already been plucked or had fallen off.

In my drugged haze, I believed this image to be spectacular. In hindsight I can see why some creative types might think that taking LSD would give them good ideas, but my bet is that the side effects are much more problematic than any ideas they might dream up. I'll take my God-given talents, thank you very much. I'm not keen on the aftereffects.

My nurse was a man named Neil who was very helpful and caring. When I was awake enough to talk he asked me if I thought I might like some breakfast. "What time is it?" I asked.

"Seven o'clock," he said, "On Saturday morning."

We agreed that I might try a liquid breakfast, which meant water, jello, and some kind of icy treat in a cup with a peel-back lid. I must have spent fifteen minutes trying to peel back the seal on that lid. My fingers wouldn't work right, I couldn't see, and I was generally useless. But at least I was trying to do something. Getting that lid peeled back became The Most Important Task In The Universe.

I finally got it open, managed to grasp a spoon, and take a slurp. It was tasty, a lemony concoction that was cold and tangy and sweet. I realized I was hungry. I tried to read the label on the lid to see what it was I was eating. No dice. My eyes felt like they were rolling like the tumblers on a slot machine. Nothing would stand still long enough for me to get a chance to look at it. The dietary department had also printed out what looked like an adding machine tape that I assumed had my "menu" printed on it. Reading that was also impossible.

I gave up and ate my jello.

Neil asked if I was ready to try getting into a chair. I was skeptical. After all, I was feeling fairly well beaten up. "You'll be surprised," he said. "I think you can do it."

A recliner was wheeled beside the bed. Neil and some other people arranged the various tubes and wires that were coming out of various parts of my body so they wouldn't get tangled up, and we gave it a try.

With a lot of assistance from my nursing team, I was able to stand briefly to move to the chair. I was quite wobbly and the effort completely exhausted me, but I got settled into a semi-seated position in the recliner. Wow! That was the first major step on the road to recovery.

Dr. Dimeling, the surgeon, stopped in to check on me. He said I had come through the surgery well but asked me how I was feeling.

"Like I've been hit by a truck," I replied.

"That's a common experience," he said and encouraged me to use the incentive spirometer. I told him Neil had already had me using it. "I can't inhale very much," I said. I was able to do 2,750 before the surgery. Now I can only do 750."

"Keep working at it," he said. "You'll find you can do more and more each day, but you have to keep at it. We don't want you to develop pneumonia. But you really are doing very well," he reassured me.

I was keeping an eye on the big clock on the wall. It was almost 8:00 AM and I was fervently hoping for what actually did happen. Charlie walked in.

All I said was, "Oh, I'm so glad to see you." She crossed from the door and cradled my head in her arms. I was overwhelmed. The last time I had seen her I wasn't sure I would see her again this side of Heaven. Yet here she was, in the flesh. And here I was, all beaten up, to be sure, but alive and even sitting in a chair. Things were looking up.

The emotions that washed over me were strong and silent. This woman—whom I loved and who loved me, with whom I had built a life, the mother of my children, the mate of my soul—was here. We were back together again. The secret loneliness I had been harboring began to leak away like floodwaters washing away downstream.

Neil provided Charlie with a chair and she immediately began to make friends. I realized how much I had learned from her. My penchant for asking the various people who worked on me about their lives came directly from watching Charlie. She knows how to engage people, and she is genuinely interested in their stories. She aways finds some connection with anyone she meets. It is an important gift and I'm happy that a little bit of it rubbed off onto me.

We met Johnnie from housekeeping. Charlie and I both liked her very much. We discovered that she was a church-going woman who taught Sunday School. She took her job of cleaning patient rooms very seriously, taking the admonition to heart that, whatever she did, she was doing it as for the Lord. We both have tremendous respect for people who do their jobs well, regardless of how lofty or menial the job may seem.

I saw Johnnie several times during my stay. She always had a pleasant word and a smile.

I also met someone from pulmonology. I'm sure her job was very important for post-surgery patients like me, but there wasn't much that I needed. I never did learn the name of this young, attractive respiratory therapist, because there was never anything she could do for me. I had an oxygen cannula in my nose and my oxygen level was in the acceptable range — above 90% — so there wasn't much else to do. Over the course of my stay she came by my room twice a day. We always waved to each other, but she was able to move on to other patients who needed her more.

Charlie gave me all the news. She said she'd seen Dr. Dimeling coming out of CCU and had been able to get an update from him. He had confirmed to her what he'd told me, that I was doing well.

She gave me a rundown of how yesterday had gone from her perspective. The boys had stayed with her all day and had only gone home after she had gotten settled back in the hotel. She had checked out this morning after having breakfast in the room using the food supplies she'd bought on Thursday night.

She told me she had sent text messages to key friends to let them know I'd come through the surgery successfully. I particularly appreciated that as I was in no condition to be trying to communicate with people. She indicated that a very large number of people, even people in other states and some foreign countries, had been praying for me.

I secretly watched her as she kept her vigil in the rather uncomfortable chair at my bedside. Perhaps the surgery had made me unusually emotional, but I welled up with tears of gratitude just being able to see her face and hear her voice.

Lunch came. By now my eyes had settled down a bit and I was able to read the paper strip that came with the meal. Apparently I had graduated to solid food and was being offered beef stroganoff. Again, I felt ravenously hungry and ate most of it.

CCU is a constant flow of personnel monitoring vital signs, checking on the patient's status, and providing services like respiratory therapy, housekeeping, food service, and physical therapy. The old joke about being woken up to take a sleeping pill isn't far from the truth. Nevertheless, I felt well cared for.

The pain level was not unbearable, but I was frequently offered pain medications. I had been told it was important to stay ahead of the pain, not to wait until I really needed something. Still, I'm not a big fan of medication of any kind, so I had to humble myself to follow the doctor's and nurse's advice. I was in a very different place than I had been just two short days ago.

No longer was I a business owner making decisions about how best to serve customers and manage cash flow. No longer was I a Sunday School teacher making preparations to ensure I was able to present the Bible as clearly and effectively as possible next Sunday. I was still a husband and father, of course, but my ability to provide good counsel or an empathetic ear was severely curtailed. I was a patient, completely in the care of the professionals who surrounded me. They knew a thousand times more about what was happening to me and what needed to be done in this situation or with that particular vital sign than I ever would. I had to trust them, that they had my best interests at heart and that they knew what they were doing. And I did trust them.

One thing we learned had to do with glucose levels. The nurses monitored my blood glucose rather carefully and several times gave me an insulin shot in my belly or in my thigh. I'd never had any indications of being diabetic. Was this an unexpected consequence of the surgery?

One nurse explained that a study done in the 1970s found that patients who had undergone major surgery often experienced increased sugar levels. "The study found an increased risk of infection with higher glucose levels," she explained. "So we monitor your glucose and, if it seems to be getting a bit high, we bring it down with a small dose of insulin. Basically we're trying to protect you from infection." The things you learn while recovering from open heart surgery.

Charlie and I have always felt that a patient in a hospital needs an advocate. We'd experienced that need when both of her parents had to be hospitalized toward the ends of their lives. Now Charlie was serving as that advocate for me, although nothing in the CCU caused us any worries.

I took stock of the "invasions" into my body. Starting at my head and working my way down, I had an oxygen cannula in my nose delivering extra oxygen to my lungs that were not quite up to speed yet. I had a complicated port just below my left clavicle. I never was sure what all it did, but it appeared to be monitoring many different parameters in my blood stream. It was also the port through which some medications were introduced into my body. On my left arm was a blood pressure cuff that inflated automatically every 15 minutes to check my blood pressure. On my left index finger was an oxygen meter that was connected by wire to the massive display up above my bed. The display showed all my vital signs and was the focus of just about anyone who came into the room. From it, they could tell how I was doing. There was another port or monitor in my right wrist. Again, I wasn't complete sure of its purpose. There was a mass of bandages on my chest that I didn't even want to think about. EKG leads also dotted the landscape on my chest. Lower on my abdomen were four drainage tubes. These connected to two plastic containers with markings on the side that allowed the nurse to have a very specific idea of how much fluid was draining out of my chest. Even further down was a Foley catheter, alleviating any worries about needing to make an impossible trip to the bathroom. I was told by one nurse that this was a fancy catheter; not only did it allow urine to pass from the bladder into a collection bag, it also measured the temperature of the urine to provide the most accurate indication of any fever I might have.

I wasn't conscious of all of these tubes and monitors all at once. They gradually made their presence known as I was slowly distanced from the trauma of having my chest opened up and my cardiac vessels rerouted.

One thing I did notice that was troublesome was that two fingers on both hands, the ring finger and the pinky, were completely numb. It felt very odd not being able to feel anything with those digits. I worried that this was a permanent side effect of the surgery and wondered how I would be able to type on a computer keyboard with numb fingers.

Another thing that was difficult was coughing. Neil encouraged me to cough as another way to keep my lungs opening up. But the pain of flexing my chest was almost unbearable. I was given a small pillow, almost like a doll's pillow, and was told to hold it tightly to my chest when I needed to cough. This was supposed to make coughing easier. I didn't find it helped much at all and grew to dread any tickle in the back of my throat.

Neil came in and wondered if I would like to try to stand up. This was to be my first physical therapy experience. "We'd just like you to stand up for a little bit. Nothing too strenuous; we don't want you to try to walk. It would just be good to change your position."

I was willing to try. With some effort and a lot of help from both Neil and Charlie, I managed to get into a standing position. My legs were wobbly and the exertion was intense, but I stood there, shaking and shivering for perhaps 30 seconds.

"OK," said Neil, "That's enough. That's really good." They eased me back down into the chair. In a way, I was discouraged. If just simply standing for half a minute was that difficult, how would I ever recover completely?

Quench not the Spirit, I preached to myself. *Let the Spirit work. In your time, Lord. Teach me to be patient.*

Late in the afternoon Neil delivered some bad news. Usually after 24 hours in the CCU, patients were ready to go to a regular room in the hospital. He thought I was ready to go, but, unfortunately, there were no beds available. I was going to have to stay another night in the CCU.

In a way that was good; I'd get another night of stellar, Cadillac level care. The bad news was that Charlie couldn't stay with me. We had planned that, once I went to a regular room, Charlie would be able to stay in the room with me. This was not allowed in the CCU.

What should Charlie do? Drive home to Berea, then drive back again tomorrow morning? I wasn't in favor of that. It is a long drive on a very busy interstate and I knew she must be exhausted. What about the hotel? Could she get another night at the hotel?

Right about that time John Paul called to check on us. After giving him an update on how I was doing, Charlie asked him if he would mind contacting the hotel to see if we could get a reservation for another night. He was very agreeable and said he'd call back when it was all arranged.

In a few minutes he called to give Charlie the confirmation number. Later we learned that he had pre-paid for the room; we never saw a bill.

Meanwhile supper came. It was turkey breast, dressing, and green beans. I ate with gusto, again surprised at my appetite and how good hospital food tasted. I had expected it to be fairly awful. It wasn't at all.

At 5:00 PM, Charlie had to leave. I hated to see her go, but begged her to get some rest. I knew it would be difficult, sleeping alone in a strange hotel.

But she needed to take care of herself. I would do my best to take care of myself, but I had lots of help. She would be alone.

The shift changed. Neil was gone and the night RN came on duty. I kick myself now because I cannot remember her name. I know she was from southern Ohio, right on the Ohio river, and that she was engaged to be married to an insurance adjustor. She was a quiet, sweet young woman who was efficient and caring, the perfect nurse for the night shift.

I tried to sleep. Honestly, though, the blood pressure cuff inflating on my arm every fifteen minutes made that an exercise in futility.

On top of that, the oxygen monitor on my finger kept malfunctioning and causing an alarm on the big panel above the bed. My new nurse would dutifully come into the room and check; every time it was a problem with the monitor, not the fact that my oxygen level was dropping.

I cat napped occasionally.

I could hear the alarms from other patients' rooms in the CCU as well. I began to concoct a bizarre scenario in my head. The periodic buzzes coming from the other rooms sounded like katydids in a Kentucky woods during a summer night. Occasionally there was a high pitched alarm that lasted longer; that was a cicada. And other noises easily became a barking dog or even a howling coyote. It was more annoying than entertaining listening to all of those players in the soundscape, but it passed the time.

My quiet nurse would tiptoe in periodically, usually to monitor my drainage tubes. I tried to always speak to her. She always apologized for waking me and said I was a very light sleeper. *I'm not a light sleeper*, I thought, *I'm a non-sleeper with all these night noises*.

One time she asked me if I had any advice for her and her fiancé about marriage, seeing as how I had a 47 year head start. "Put your husband ahead of yourself," I said, "As he should put you ahead of himself. And always keep Christ in the center."

"Good advice," she said.

The clock slowly crept around, fifteen minutes between blood pressure cuff inflations, and finally it was morning.

Breakfast was comprised of rather uninspiring scrambled eggs and toast. It was the first meal I wasn't thrilled about. But I was intrigued by the presence of another cup of the icy treat that had given me such a challenge the previous morning. This time I was able to read the label — it was some kind of sorbet

— and to peel back the cover. It was almost as refreshing as it had been the previous morning.

Dr. Dimeling returned to check on his patient. He again expressed his satisfaction at how well I was doing. He noted that my blood pressure was coming up well and that my oxygen level was holding steady. He said, "We'll get you up for a walk today." *Well, OK,* I thought. *If you think I can I'll give it a try when the time comes.* He remarked that the arteries supplying blood to my heart were now completely repaired, but that the healing of my sternum was going to take some time. "We slit your sternum down the middle," he said. "It takes a while for the bones to fuse together again. Meanwhile, I wired your sternum together."

"Wires?" I asked. I always want to learn more.

"Yes," he said, picking up a dry erase marker and stepping to the white board where the nurses recorded who were my key caregivers. He started to sketch with a purple marker. "Your breast bone is actually comprised of three bones," he said, deftly sketching what looked to me like a very detailed model. "This is the manubrium," he said, sketching a six sided object. "Here is the main part of the sternum, and this is the xiphoid process." He indicated a small three sided object at the bottom of the sternum. "The ribs come off here, here and here …" He sketched a beautiful set of ribs, like he could draw them in his sleep. "I drilled holes through your manubrium here, here and here. Then I threaded a titanium wire through the holes and tightened them to keep your bones in place and in line. I also looped three more here, here and here around the bone." He indicated three places lower down on my sternum.

"I'll bet my x-ray is going to look strange from now on."

He chuckled. "Yes, it will."

"How do you tighten up the wires?"

"Well," he laughed. "Kind of like tightening up using a pair of pliers." I suspected the pliers were a bit more sophisticated than the rusty pair I had at home, but I got the idea. "We just want you to be very, very careful to not do anything that might cause the bones to shift. We need to give them time — two months at least — to really start knitting back together."

"I was told I have to sleep on my back."

"Yes. Sleeping on your side would put a torque on your sternum. That wouldn't be good. I also don't want you lifting more than five pounds."

"Five pounds is less than a gallon of milk."

"You're right. A gallon weighs about eight pounds. It won't be easy, but I want you to be very intentional about being careful with your sternum, OK?"

"OK," I agreed. "By the way, Doc, I used to travel a lot. I guess I'll set off the scanners at the airport now, huh?"

"No, I used titanium wires. They're non-ferrous. Beside, people at the airport know what to look for. The scar on your chest will be a giveaway."

We chatted a bit more before he moved on to his next patient. I was left with a very accurate sketch of a breastbone and ribs, along with six sets of wires holding things together. More than once I looked at the diagram, fixing in my mind what my insides must look like.

The shift changed again. My quiet night nurse was replaced by a young RN named Ryley. She seemed about the same age as the previous nurse, but she was married to an optometrist. She had long, dark hair and was every bit as efficient as Julianne, Neil, and my unnamed friend from the night before. The staff in the CCU was absolutely top notch.

Charlie arrived promptly at 8:00 AM. "Has Dr. Dimeling been in?" she asked.

"Yes, he was here about 20 minute ago." I pointed to the diagram of the sternum and ribs. "He showed me where he put the wires in to hold my chest together. How did your night at the hotel go?"

She admitted to not sleeping terribly well, but she had managed to get some breakfast and had checked out again this morning. We hoped that I would be moved to a regular room today so that she could stay with me in the hospital.

Ryley was sympathetic to our planning. "We do like to get our cabbage patients out of the CCU by the second day, for sure," she agreed. "But the hospital is very full right now. I understand they're having a hard time finding you a room. But I do know that you're high priority; they want to get you moved if they can. It will just depend on what comes in through the ER and admitting. You're in good shape here, so please don't worry."

"Y'all are taking very good care of my husband," Charlie said. "But I'd like to be able to stay with him rather than having to get a hotel again."

"I completely understand," Ryley replied. "I'll keep you informed. Usually we see a transition around noon. If they haven't found you a room by about 3:00 when there is a shift change, it probably isn't going to happen. So we'll keep an eye on the situation."

"Thanks, Ryley," I said. "But I have to ask. You called me a cabbage patient, what did you mean?"

"That's what you had done," she said. "You had a CABG procedure." This time she spelled it out. CABG sounds like "cabbage" when you say it.

"What's CABG? I thought I had bypass surgery. Six of them, by the way."

She laughed. "Oh, you did. CABG stands for Coronary Artery Bypass Graft. That's exactly what you had: bypass surgery, more accurately known as CABG."

"Hmm," I said. "So now I have a cabbage heart, I guess!"

"I guess!" she replied.

Mid morning two physical therapists arrived, saying they'd like to take me for a walk. I was eager to get mobile, and was becoming heartily sick of the recliner I'd been in for more than 24 hours now, but I wasn't sure how well I'd be able to perform.

The preparations were elaborate. With all my tubes and hoses, it took some doing to get the IV bags on a pole that could roll along with me. The drainage tubes and their containers had to be hung from a walker that I would be holding on to, along with the Foley catheter bag. When we were all set up, the two ladies helped me to stand up. It was a little easier than yesterday, although I was still quite shaky. "Whenever you're ready," the physical therapist said.

We headed out. It was quite a parade. First came the walker with various bags and bottles hanging on it. Then came me, hanging on to the walker. To my side was the physical therapist, hanging on to me and bringing along the IV pole. Behind me came my recliner, being wheeled from behind with the PT assistant. Charlie served as drum major from the sidelines.

Each step was a major ordeal, a real accomplishment when I'd managed to shuffle one foot out in front of me. The pain was fairly significant all over, but particularly in my chest. We turned left out of the door of my room and headed into the corridor. I could see the doors of other rooms, but couldn't really see the patients inside. Somewhere along the line Ryley joined the parade. She wanted to check my oxygen level since we'd left the wired O_2 meter back in the room. She used a little hand-held unit and discovered my oxygen level was dropping significantly. I began to shake uncontrollably and my forehead became covered with sweat. Still I kept going, or at least I tried to.

We had advanced a few feet down the hall so that we were at the nurse's station. "I think you'd better sit down," said the physical therapist. "We need to get you on some oxygen." I sank into the recliner while the PT assistant kept it from sliding. A nurse I didn't know found a small fan and turned it on my face. That helped; I was beginning to feel a bit faint. Someone else brought a bottle of oxygen and fitted my nose with a cannula to get the O_2 started.

After a few minutes, the physical therapist asked how I was feeling. "I bit better," I replied weekly.

"Ok, good. Your oxygen level is looking better. We'll wheel you back to your room now. That's enough for one day."

"No," I said. "I started this. I'd like to try to finish it."

"Well, I like your attitude," she replied. "Are you sure?" I nodded.

So the parade began again, this time with even more staff in attendance and an oxygen bottle on wheels joining in.

The bad news was that I was still very weak and in pain. But the good news was that I was able to complete the full circuit around the nurse's station and back to my room without collapsing in the hallway. I sank gratefully into my chair back in my room while everyone expressed how pleased they were that I'd been able to complete the walk.

I, too, was happy I'd done it, but it reinforced to me how far I had to go. If a little walk a few yards around the hallway was that difficult, what chance did I have of being able to resume any kind of normal life?

I'm sure I napped after that — although I was reconnected to all the monitors, including the despised blood pressure cuff that inflated like clockwork every 15 minutes.

Charlie, my champion and fearless defender, waited patiently by my side.

Lunch arrived. It was some excuse for goulash. Suddenly my appetite was gone. I tried to eat a few bites, but the eagerness with which I had eaten my first few meals had evaporated. Food now turned my stomach.

It was a long boring afternoon. I continued to sleep off and on, and we were visited by a procession of professionals, each doing their part to further my recovery. Johnnie from housekeeping came by. Ryley checked on me frequently. The silent respiratory therapist waved from the hallway as there was nothing she could provide that I really needed. The blood pressure cuff kept its inflation cadence every 15 minutes. And, just to liven things up, the oxygen meter would set off an alarm saying my O_2 level was dangerously low. Each time it was a malfunction of the device on my finger, not a real problem. The only oxygen problem I had was when I tried that first walk in the hallway.

As it neared 3:00, Ryley came in with the bad news. There were still no beds available in the regular part of the hospital. It looked like I would be spending yet another night in the CCU. In terms of the care I was receiving that would be great. But it was Charlie I was worried about. We had decided that perhaps she should go home tonight to get fresh clothes and check on things at the house. She could take her time about coming back tomorrow morning since I seemed to be doing reasonably well. Neither of us liked that solution, but it seemed like the best idea. Charlie began gathering her things together to leave.

Ryley came in again. "I sort of got the idea you were getting ready to leave," she said to Charlie. "So I thought I'd better come and tell you. They've found you a room on 3rd floor. You'll be moving the a hospital room after all!"

Suddenly we were preparing to relocate.

"You've been doing very well and your vitals are all good," Ryley told me. "But before you can go, I need to remove several of your tubes. We don't send patients up to the floor with those."

She set to work. Out came the subclavian artery port with all of its attachments and tubes. I expected that one to be painful, but it slid out without a problem. The monitoring line in my wrist also came out. Off came the oxygen monitor on my finger. I wasn't sad to see it go because it had given false alarms for more than a day. Off came the despised blood pressure cuff. From now on a nurse or an aide would be taking my blood pressure the old fashioned way.

And then Ryley announced that the Foley catheter would also come out. I had mixed feelings about that. I would be happy to have fewer tubes but I knew that meant I was now responsible for letting someone know when I needed to use the bathroom. "They'll provide you with a urinal bottle on the floor," Ryley assured me.

The only tubes left were my IV and the four drainage tubes coming out of my chest. "When do you think I might get those to come out?" I asked. I was particularly interested because, of all the tube and monitors, those were the most painful.

"That will be the doctor's call," said Ryley. "You're still producing enough fluid that I don't think they'll come out quite yet, but the amount is decreasing steadily so it might be in the next day or two."

Ryley brought in a wheelchair and proceeded to move my remaining connections to my new conveyance. Charlie gathered up her things, and we were ready to go to my new room on the 3rd floor.

Hospital

My new location was less than stellar. Where the CCU had been state of the art, my new quarters felt like they were stuck in the 1970s. The room was small. Thankfully it was a single room. (I had suddenly thought, *what if I have a roommate*, as Ryley wheeled me off of the elevator.). There was a bathroom on the left as you entered the room, then a single hospital bed and a recliner against the window. There wasn't room for anything else. There were lots of windows with a lovely view of a commercial air conditioning unit on the roof of the adjacent building. At least I could see the sky and the big puffy cumulous clouds sailing by. A little card in the windowsill said that my room had been cleaned by Thomas. *I'll have to thank Thomas when I see him*, I thought, in keeping with my belief in not quenching the Spirit. A sink unit occupied the wall closer to the doorway. It looked like something inspired by the Jetsons, then left unchanged for the last 40 years.

Charlie and I had decided that it would be best for me to stay in the recliner since I dared not twist in bed or sleep on my side for fear of damaging my sternum. She would attempt to sleep in the bed. She tested the mattress; it was a major step down from the hotel room bed she'd been in the night before. But at least we would be together. After seeing me settled in the recliner, Ryley bid us farewell and wished us a continued good recovery.

The head nurse came in and introduced herself to us, asking if there was anything she could do. We didn't know enough to ask for anything. The nurses and staff in the CCU had been so efficient and caring that we didn't know what we might be missing. We would find out as the night progressed.

The nurse who had charge of my case also came in. She was rushed and brusk. Did I need anything for pain? *Maybe; I wasn't sure yet.* Had I had dinner? *No.* She would be sending in an aide to get my vitals. *OK.* Use the call button if I needed something; she had other patients to attend to.

The aide who was to take my vitals came in. She took my blood pressure the old fashioned way as expected. She also took my temperature. That was new; the high tech equipment in the CCU had done that automatically. She clipped the oxygen meter on my finger. That was better; no false reading this time. "I guess I'll need a urinal bottle," I said, thinking I'd better be proactive about asking for that rather than waiting until I really needed to go.

The aid was a nice young woman but clearly overworked. I don't know how many patients she had to tend to, but she was the type of person who did what needed to be done, then moved on to the next task. "I'll see about asking dietary to bring you some dinner," she said. By now it was about 6:30 PM on Sunday night.

Dinner came. It was some inedible attempt at tortillas, perhaps masquerading as a quesadilla. My appetite fled. In fact, unlike the first day in CCU, I was now struggling to choke down anything. It all seemed repulsive.

The phlebotomist came in to draw blood. That was a new experience. The subclavian artery port I'd had in the CCU was used whenever a blood sample was needed. Now I would have to submit to being stuck by a needle in the arm.

Charlie reminded me that often the third day after surgery is the worst. She had the belief that by the third day, the major anesthesia and pain medications are wearing off enough that the reality of what has been done to the patient's body really begins to be felt. Tomorrow would be the third day. Her thoughts turned out to be prophetic.

It wasn't an easy night. My pain did intensify. Apparently the doctor's orders were that the nurse could not administer pain medication when she saw I needed it. I had to specifically ask for it. There was a tug-of-war in my mind: was asking for pain medication a sign of weakness? Was I in danger of becoming too dependent on it? Or was it wiser to stay ahead of the pain so that it did not become all-consuming and prevent my body from much needed rest and healing?

In the end I did ask for medication several times; once or twice it was given as injectable morphine. While morphine did help to dull the pain, it also made me feel strange. I wasn't a fan.

Meanwhile Charlie was trying to make do with a hospital bed that had lots of buttons for raising this and lowering that, but that did not seem designed for comfort. It had some kind of air mattress that we figured was intended to inflate or deflate automatically based on the sleeper's position. It had a mind of its own, acting like an overinflated air mattress at one moment, then suddenly losing all of its air so that Charlie felt like she was sleeping on a board.

It wasn't an easy night for either one of us.

Because the port had been taken out, checking my glucose level meant a finger stick to get a drop of blood. The aide was a frequent visitor to our room to check my sugar, or to take a blood pressure, or to verify my oxygen level, or take my temperature. My fingers began to get sensitive from all of the poking.

The numbness in my two little fingers, particularly on my right hand, continued to plague and worry me.

As feared, urination became my own personal responsibility. I had been given a urine bottle and, several times during the night, I had to make use of it, adjusting in the recliner and pushing sheets around so that I could take care of business.

My nurse for the day shift was an interesting man named Josh. Like so many others, he was a traveling nurse, not on staff at the hospital but traveling to where he was needed. Through the course of the day we had many conversations with Josh and learned a lot about him. Unlike the RN on duty through the night, he seemed quite happy to spend time with his patients.

Josh and his wife were both "travelers" — as these contract workers are often called. They had been assigned to Lexington for several months. Prior to that, they had been on a multi-month trip out west. That led to conversations about our trip out west and the fortuitous discovery of my need for open heart surgery as a result of getting short of breath in Yellowstone.

"Have you ever thought about getting a fifth wheel and going on the road for an extended time?" Josh asked. That we had enjoyed our trip out west came through in the conversation; we had that in common.

"No," Charlie said. "I'm not into camping." She described her childhood in East Tennessee in which she had not had running water in her home until age six. "I grew up with an outhouse," she told Josh. "I have no desire to go back to that kind of lifestyle."

Josh laughed. "Oh, you don't have the right idea about camping these days. In my fifth wheel we have a full size bathroom. The shower is big enough for me and my wife at the same time. I've got a full size recliner and a large flat screen TV. The bed is a full size queen. My wife and I both love to cook; we've got all we need to get creative in the kitchen."

It turned out that, while they were originally from Florida, they had no home now. Instead, this fifth wheel camper was their home. They just pulled it wherever they were working, or, when they weren't, headed out on the road to visit places they wanted to go. Apparently the pay for a traveling nurse was so good that they could afford to maintain this kind of lifestyle.

Later on in the day Josh did tell us that he owned a cattle farm in North Carolina. When we finally got around to asking where in North Carolina, we learned that Josh's farm was in Cherokee County, the same county where I had grown up and gone through high school.

Josh was a good distraction for me as a patient. He was a capable nurse, too. His worldview was different from ours, though. We asked him about his religious faith because he seemed to exemplify tolerant hedonism. He said that he was very happy for people to believe whatever they wanted, but he didn't have much use for it himself.

I was glad for the distraction provided by Josh because I wasn't feeling very well. Charlie's prediction about the third day was coming to pass. At one point I felt quite nauseated. At another point I tried to go to the bathroom, but that proved too painful. The four drainage tubes in my chest were really beginning to hurt.

Apparently there was some kind of checklist of things that an open heart surgery patient should be able to do before they can be sent home. Sit in a chair, check. Stand unassisted, check. Keep food down, check. Pass urine, check. Walk a certain distance, not yet. Have a bowel movement, not yet. All external tubes removed, no, because I still had the chest tubes. I wasn't sure what other things were on the list, but I was beginning to get interested in being able to go home.

My appetite still wasn't good, even though I had eaten several meals and the "keep food down" box had been checked off. The dietary people would announce themselves and, with a flourish, the name of the tempting cuisine they were setting before me. None of it was in the least bit enticing.

A new lady named Carol from Physical Therapy came by and wanted me to take a walk. Based on the experience in the Cardiac Care Unit I had the day before, my expectations weren't very high. But Carol was good at motivation and kept a close watch on me with a belt looped around me in case I began to fall. Josh had told me earlier that I was, under no circumstances, to fall while under his care. "I don't know how to fill out the paperwork," he said. "So you won't be falling."

With Carol's help I managed to walk down to the end of the short hall and back without having to stop. I was actually making some progress.

My love/hate relationship with the incentive spirometer grew more pronounced. Each day I had been able to add a little bit to my lung capacity, but I was still well under half of my original capacity. Josh encouraged me to take deep breaths. I understood the concept, but my body wasn't capable. The pain would shoot through my chest when I tried to breathe deeply. Josh pointed out that, once I got the chest tubes out, I would probably feel quite a bit better.

Pastor Greg came for a visit. I wasn't as conversational as I would have liked because I just didn't feel very good. But I really did appreciate him coming.

Later in the day our son Mark stopped in. He brought a present from a lady in my Sunday School class, wrapped in pretty paper. It was a hand bell along with a note that said I was to use the bell to summon Charlie when I needed something. It was a thoughtful and humorous gift.

As Mark and I talked, he said something that really struck me. "Dad," he said. "The way you're talking it is almost as if you are disappointed that you made it through the surgery."

I had to think about that. Finally, I answered, "I suppose, in some ways, I am. I would have hated to have to leave you and your brothers, your Mom and the grandkids. But I would not have missed this sinful, messed up world. I would have been glad to go and be with the Lord, to go to my rest, and not have to deal with all of this. So, yes, in a strange way, I guess I am disappointed." We both pondered on that for a few minutes. Then I added, "God appears to have spared my life for a reason. What that reason is, is unclear to me now. But I'm praying that, as I recover, the path God has for me will become obvious."

The second night in the hospital room was similar to the first night. I was coughing more, which the staff said was a good thing; it would expel residual mucus in my lungs. I then learned that sneezing was twice as painful as coughing. The doll pillow did little to alleviate the pain. I think the theory is that, by pressing on my sternum with the pillow, I could balance the pressure coming from the inside when I coughed or sneezed. I never got the hang of it.

The second night was just as rough for Charlie, too. Several times we had to explain to someone that the patient was the guy in the recliner, not the woman in the hospital bed. If they must draw blood, they should get it from me, not from Charlie.

The finger sticks continued as a way to monitor my glucose, but my sugar seemed to be well controlled — I didn't need any insulin after the two days in the CCU.

There were some indications that I might be sent home on Tuesday. That seemed premature to us because I was extremely weak and still in a fair amount of pain. I thought I might be able to use the bathroom, but the effort of getting to sit on the toilet was painful. I had to bring along the drainage containers and, once I was on the throne, the pain of those tubes poking inside my chest was unbearable. I had to be helped back to bed, leaving the "had a bowel movement" box still unchecked. Maybe I wouldn't be going home so soon after all.

On Tuesday morning we met our new RN for the day. Julie had been the Director of Nursing at a long term care facility in Corbin, Kentucky before coming to Saint Joe. She had harrowing stories to tell about the Covid pandemic and how her facility was forced to handle it. She said that, when the Governor first announced that nursing homes were to be cut off from any interaction with the outside world, she couldn't believe it. "Our residents needed to see their families more than anything. I told them that isolation will be a death sentence for many," she said. Her words proved to be prophetic.

"Then," she said, "The government began paying people the stimulus money. I went to our chief administrator and said, 'What are we going to do? People will stay home; they're being paid not to work.' We ended up having to pay more than people could make by not working, and that drove up the cost of nursing home care. We still barely survived with a skeleton crew. Those were really bad times, and some of the things the government did made it worse, much worse, for both our patients and our staff."

I was interested in Julie's perspective, but she had a bigger patient load than Josh had had the previous day. She was attentive when I needed her, but she didn't have as much time to stay and chat.

Carol from Physical Therapy returned and asked if I was up for a longer walk. I thought it would be good to try, and this time we walked the entire circuit around both sides of the floor. Where the day before I had walked to the end of the hall and back, this time I was able to walk what was probably four or five times that distance.

It did seem I was making some progress.

I learned Carol's story as we walked. She was originally from Michigan, had been to Kentucky on vacation one year. When she divorced her husband, she decided to move here. "Best move I ever made," she said. Her adult children had seen how satisfied she was in the Bluegrass State, and they had each ended up moving to Kentucky as well. Ultimately even her own parents decided to make the move. "Now we're all here together in Kentucky," she said.

One incident marred our walk. As Carol was shepherding me down the back hall, a woman in scrubs walked briskly past us heading in the opposite direction. "He should be wearing a mask," she said curtly to Carol. That's all she said; she kept on walking past us. Carol didn't comment. It was true, I was not wearing a mask, nor had I at any time in the hospital, because I needed the oxygen cannula in my nose. A mask would have jeopardized my ability to breathe and maintain my blood oxygen level. I thought it odd that this woman, without knowing anything about my specific medical condition, felt it necessary to point out an infraction I was committing and that, by extension, Carol was allowing me to commit. I followed Carol's example and ignored the woman's comment.

The weather outside was outstanding. Because my chair was right by the window, I had a direct view framed between the two high-rise parts of the hospital. If I overlooked the air conditioning units in the foreground, the sky was a sight to behold. It was a deep, late-summer blue, dotted with puffy clouds. Occasionally the clouds would have shadows within shadows; I loved watching their subtle and changing hues of white, creams and grays. When I felt better, I thought, I might take up my watercolors again and see if I could do a cloud. I knew from experience that seeing something and then reproducing it with independent-minded watercolor paints were two entirely different things.

Still, I loved looking at God's creation and His color schemes and compositions, even as I contemplated strategies for painting something similar. Even more importantly, looking at the sky and the clouds gave me peace and comfort.

❦

I was lying in my recliner and Charlie was sitting in the guest chair, when there was a knock on the door. "Housekeeping," said a male voice.

"Come in," we both said together.

"Hello, I am Thomas," said the man who entered. "Will it be all right if I clean your room?"

"Of course," we said. And I added, "Are you the Thomas who cleaned the room before I got here?" I indicated the little card that had been left in the windowsill.

"Yes, I am Thomas," he said. He was not a tall man and his skin was dark as ebony. He had on a surgical mask (as all the healthcare staff did) so that only his dancing eyes could be seen above the edge. There was something about him that drew me.

His accent sounded African to me, and I asked him where he was from.

"From Ghana," he said. Gradually, as he worked, his story came out. He had come to the United States 14 years ago and very much hoped, someday, to be able to attend college. He was charming, humble, and friendly.

When he had finished cleaning, he said, "Sir, I wish for you a very good recovery."

"Thank you," I said. "God is good."

His eyes snapped wide and he looked intently at me. "God is good all the time!"

"Yes He is!"

Charlie asked, "Thomas, do you attend church somewhere?"

"Oh, yes ma'am. I attend the Consolidated Baptist Church. Do you know it?"

We didn't, although we later learned that this was a fairly large church comprised mostly of African expatriates.

"Before I go," Thomas said, "May I pray for you? I feel the Spirit telling me to pray, and I must not quench the Spirit."

"I would be grateful if you would," I said.

Thus began what for both Charlie and me was most likely the pinnacle of our hospital experience. This gentle man from Africa began to pray. His hands were raised toward Heaven. He began to rock back and forth as the rhythm of the prayer began to pervade the room. He began to cry as he begged the Lord for swift healing for me. He began to laugh as he felt the confirmation of the Holy Spirit. Through this anointed man I felt as if we were transported into the very throne room of Heaven.

The Spirit within me responded. I, too, was reaching my hands toward Heaven. The "Amen!" and "Yes, Lord!" on my lips were a counterpoint to Thomas' powerful prayer. We were having church in that cramped hospital room being led by this man of God.

Thomas finished his prayer and looked at both of us. His eyes were wet with tears, and I guess mine were too. Looking into his eyes, there was a connection between us that can only be forged between people who are both citizens of the Kingdom of God. In the world's eyes, Thomas and I were very different. But we both knew that we were brothers.

Thomas looked at Charlie. "I can't go out there like this," he said, indicating his tear-stained eyes. "They mustn't see me this way." Charlie got him some tissues, but before he could dry his eyes, he was moved to pray again. Again we were transported into the Lord's presence through Thomas' fervent prayer. Again my Spririt responded. I didn't want it to stop; I could feel the healing of my body increasing as Thomas interceded for me.

When he was finished, Thomas began to wipe his eyes with the tissue Charlie had given him. From my vantage point by the window, I could see them look at each other. Something significant passed between them and Thomas was again praying, rocking, crying, laughing, and raising his hands to God.

Finally Thomas was able to regain his composure. It had been exhilarating and energizing. I thanked Thomas from the bottom of my heart. Of all the people who had been in and out of my life over the past five days, Thomas was the most important. We shook hands. Charlie hugged him. Had I been able, I would have hugged him, too.

Part of me wants to go to the Consolidated Baptist Church on a Sunday morning and ask if anyone knows Thomas from Ghana. But an even bigger part of me doesn't need to go because I feel almost certain that Thomas was an interceding angel sent by God to strengthen me.

Whoever he was, Thomas is someone I'm going to seek out when the good Lord does finally allow me to enter into His Heaven.

A man in a lab coat introduced himself as Patrick Pepper, the Physician's Assistant associated with Dr. Dimeling. He was in his 50s with a shaved head and a big smile. "I'm here to take out your drainage tubes," he announced.

I was really pleased because the tubes were quite painful and because this was another box that must be checked before I could go home. "What a great name," I said. "Patrick Pepper! That's outstanding."

"If you like my name, you'll like my dog's name, too," he replied. "His name is Sargeant."

I'm happy to say that my brain was working well enough for me to get the Beatles reference. I laughed, but then stopped because the drainage tubes made it painful.

Patrick asked me to lie down on the bed. "Can I watch?" asked Charlie.

"Sure," said Patrick. "If you want to." I didn't think I wanted to watch myself. The thought of four tubes being pulled out of my chest cavity gave me the willies.

Patrick busied himself with getting set up. Several times Charlie handed him something he needed before he actually reached for it. "Are you a nurse?" Patrick asked.

"No, why?"

"You're anticipating what I need before I even know it," he said. He looked at her. "You're very good."

"Yes, she is," I commented. "I'm a blessed man."

"All right," said Patrick, looking at me. "Are you ready?"

"As ready as I'll ever be," I said. I was dreading this.

"OK, here we go," said Patrick. And, before I knew it, all four tubes were out. It wasn't nearly as bad as I had expected. Charlie snapped a rather grizzly photo using her phone of the four bloody drainage tubes lying on my stomach and the holes they had just been pulled out of. It was only later that she showed me the picture; that was my first inkling of how dramatic my incisions looked.

Patrick then set to work packing the four holes with bandages and redoing the dressings on my chest. Again, Charlie played the role of assisting nurse, handing him rolls of tape and scissors when he needed them.

When he was done, I smelled of antiseptic but I had nice clean gauze taped up and down my front.

"Will I get to go home today?" I asked.

"I believe you're ready to get out of here," he said. "But I don't have the final say."

Late in the afternoon yet another representative of the surgeon's staff stopped in. "I'm the one who removed the vein from your leg," she said.

"I guess I was out of it at the time," I said.

"I introduced myself to you when you first came into the operating theater," she said. "Perhaps you don't remember. I'm also the one who put in the subclavian artery port."

"You asked me to extend my arm …" I said vaguely.

"Yes, that was me," she said. "We use a fancy technique where we run a scope up through the vein in your leg so that we can follow it. That way we don't have to leave a big long scar on your thigh." Instead I had a three inch incision just below and inside my right knee and a smaller wound near the top of my thigh.

She checked my incisions in both locations and pronounced herself satisfied. "It's looking very good," she said. "So I'm going to say that you can go home."

"Really?" I was surprised.

"Yes, your drainage tubes are out, your incisions look good, your vital signs are good. You're ready to go home and start recovering in a more familiar environment."

"That's great," I said. I didn't tell her that I knew there was at least one more box to check. I had yet to successfully use the bathroom

"I'll get the paperwork started. The nurse will be in soon to coordinate your discharge."

Things began to move. Julie came in to initiate discharge proceedings. "I'm going to start working on the paperwork," she said. "Be patient. There are a lot of procedures involved."

In the midst of it all, I needed to go to the bathroom again. This time it was a success. The last box was checked. I really could go home.

Julie brought in a stack of papers — it looked like at least 50 pages. "These are your discharge orders," she said. "And we need to go over every page. But here at Saint Joe we have a special way of doing that. We call her the 'nurse on a stick.'" She wheeled in what looked a bit like an IV pole, but it had an iPad and a camera on it. She turned on the iPad and Julie explained that a discharge nurse would be going over my discharge paperwork with me. I would talk to her remotely using the "nurse on a stick."

After some delay, the iPad came to life and I could see a woman looking at me. "Hi there," she said. She introduced herself and told me she would be going over my discharge paperwork. She had a touch of a hispanic accent and she said that she was located in Texas. She wanted to know who else was in the room. When I told her Charlie was with me, she wanted to make sure I was OK with her discussing my case in front of my wife. Apparently she took privacy very seriously, but Charlie and I have always felt that two sets of ears are better than one, especially where complicated medical information is involved.

The review of the discharge paperwork was very thorough. We looked at every single page — she had an exact duplicate of my paperwork in front of her. We talked about what vital signs to watch and what to do if something went wrong. For example, she said I should expect to run a fever for a few days, but to contact our Nurse Navigator if it went over 100° F or persisted more than a few days. We talked about how to care for my surgical wounds. We talked about how vulnerable my sternum was to being injured. We talked about sleeping — no sleeping on my side, which might cause my sternum to come out of alignment or slow its healing. We talked about resuming physical exercise: very slow at first and gradually building over the course of two months. We talked about going to cardiac rehab later on to begin gaining my strength back. We went over each of my medications. We talked about diet.

She asked if any of the medications that were now on the list were new to me. Four of them were. "Our pharmacy has a service," she said. "We can have the pharmacy bring you prescriptions of the medications you don't already have. That way you can leave here with the drugs your doctor wants you to take rather than having to go to your local drug store as you go home. Would you like us to do that?"

It made sense. "Yes," we said.

"Great," she replied. "I'm putting in an order with the pharmacy right now. They should have your medications to your shortly."

When we were finished, we said goodbye to our nurse on a stick and called our son Luke.

It was getting on towards 5:00 PM and Luke would be getting off work soon. We thought it might be preferable if he could drive us home rather than Charlie braving rush hour traffic. I was not allowed to drive, nor would I be until Dr. Dimeling cleared me to do so. Luke said he would come by the hospital as soon as he got off work.

Dietary brought in another inedible sampling of their cuisine. It languished in the corner, unexamined and unappreciated. I managed to get out of my hospital gown and pull on some very loose fitting clothes in readiness for leaving.

The clock crawled forward. Luke arrived. We waited for the pharmacy people to make their delivery. After about an hour we asked Julie if she knew what the holdup was. She went to check. On returning, she said, "They say they're leaving now."

Another thirty minutes passed. I was beginning to get anxious. Julie popped her head in the room with a questioning look on her face. "Still waiting," we told her.

After a two hour wait, a young woman from pharmacy finally arrived. It marred what could have been a happy exit. Not only was the delivery much later than we expected, there were only three drugs instead of the promised four. Charlie would have to pick up the fourth one at our local pharmacy tomorrow — which rather defeated the purpose of going home with the prescriptions in hand. And then the young lady presented us with a bill. The drugs apparently were not part of my hospital stay, therefore we had to pay for them separately. "Just call us with your credit card number or put a check in the mail," the young woman said cheerfully.

Finally I was bundled into a wheelchair for the ride down to the lobby while Charlie went to get the car. We had thought about having Luke drive us home, but realized that would leave one vehicle in Lexington and then Luke would have to get from our house to his home. So we decided Charlie would drive and Luke would follow, just in case we had problems.

I eased into the back seat and placed the doll's pillow on my chest before buckling the seatbelt. Traffic wasn't terrible and I marveled at the sunshine and scenery as Charlie drove. It was good to be going home.

The trip was uneventful and I was able to walk from the car to the bedroom and the new recliner Charlie had thoughtfully suggested we buy. I was exhausted but home. I had a wife who was the center of my world and children and grandchildren who orbited that nucleus.

Charlie brought me my nighttime medications and I settled down to try to sleep in a chair.

Recovery

Thus began the long, slow slog of recovery. Looking back, it was painfully slow with progress being measured in millimeters, not miles. Three steps forward were followed by at least two or three back. At first, and for many weeks, it seemed as if I would never recover from having my chest opened to the world.

For me, the most significant challenge was sleeping in a chair. I'm a devoted side sleeper; sleeping on my back is difficult, uncomfortable, and just wrong. Thank goodness for the new chair. It forced me to sleep in this unnatural way so that my sternum would have a chance to knit back together correctly. The doctors had so thoroughly warned me about putting strain or torque on my sternum that I desperately wanted to comply, but I struggled every step of the way.

Being home was not without its bright side, however. The next morning I was able to get up and eat some breakfast. Hallelujah, my appetite had returned now that I had some food so ably fixed by my talented wife. Whatever Charlie placed before me tasted wonderful. She limited my portions and I ate everything she gave me.

My first trip to the scales was shocking; I had gained five pounds while in the hospital. I gather most of that was fluid which gradually came off during the first couple of weeks so that, by the end of the second week, I had lost about ten pounds from when I went in for surgery. So far I've managed to keep those pounds from returning and have even lost a few more, which apparently makes the doctors happy.

Something that made me happy was the color of the flowers Charlie had planted around our house. Charlie loves her flower beds and I remember gazing at the blue salvia, the red verbena, and the bright orange lantana on that first morning and being amazed at the intensity of the hues. I found great pleasure in the smallest things: the "teakettle, teakettle" call of a wren, the hum of the bumblebees as they worked over the salvia, the rustle of a breeze in the maple tree, the quiet munch, munch, munch of the grazing goats, the whir of a cicada on a fence post. In those first few weeks I was overwhelmed with the goodness of God, at His providence in both providing for my health as well as His beautiful creation.

Nothing was easy. Even the simplest tasks took planning, concentration, and a tolerance for pain. Whether it was pulling on some shoes or brushing my teeth or simply getting into or out of a chair, I had to think about it and move carefully. It got easer as the weeks went by; even months later, however, I still act with more deliberation than I used to.

Charlie took excellent care of me. She monitored every pain medication I took, making sure I took the pills on schedule so that the pain did not overcome me, and making sure I wasn't taking anything too often as we certainly didn't want me to become dependent on the powerful drugs I had been given. Charlie also monitored my temperature, my oxygen level, my blood pressure, and my pulse. Two nights in a row I had a temperature of 100.6° F. Charlie was concerned enough that she called and talked to Debbie, our "nurse navigator." Debbie was reassuring, telling Charlie that a fever the first few days was not unexpected, but that Charlie was right to monitor my temperature. If it continued we might need to intervene. Happily on the third day my temperature was closer to normal.

More than anything, Charlie was fierce and caring. She made sure I did the hard things that were needful for recovery, and she watched out for every little detail that would give me strength or encouragement for the difficult journey I was on. Of course, she was on the journey with me. I was the one doing the physical work of healing. She was carrying just as much of an emotional load as I was, if not more. My gratitude to her continues to grow daily as she exhibits the quiet strength of a partner, advocate, nurse and wife. I doubt my recovery would have stayed on track without her.

John Paul was also extremely helpful in that first week home from the hospital. Our son insisted on spending the night at our house, working remotely during the day and being available at night. He was away from his wife and six kids as he provided backup both to Charlie and to me. Jeremy was doing a great job of taking over the LAMP Consortium operations while I was out of commission; John Paul was his backup, too. Most of the time, John Paul's technical expertise and the fact that we had worked together in the past was enough to provide the help Jeremy needed. But several times in that first week John Paul had to slip into my bedroom to see if I was awake or napping. If I was awake, he would ask for some guidance about a particular issue he and Jeremy were managing. It was quite encouraging to know that things were being taken care of with such capability, but it was also nice to talk shop for a few minutes. It helped relieve the tedium of being so incapacitated.

On the second day home we decided to try doing a shower. My body still smelled of antiseptic and I was also beginning to develop the telltale odor of the unwashed. I had been told by the "nurse on a stick" that I could shower, but that I had to keep my back to the water and protect the dressing on my chest as much as possible. But the idea of washing off a bit of the hospital grime was more appealing than the challenges I would likely face.

Charlie helped immensely. The first foray into the shower was brief and shaky. I was shivering so badly after just a few minutes that I had to call it off.

The shivering wasn't from cold so much as from exhaustion; standing in the shower took every ounce of strength I had and a bit more. Charlie helped dry me off, being very careful about my incisions, and got me back into some pajamas. I headed back to my recliner for another nap.

The love/hate relationship I had with the incentive spirometer continued now that I was home. The doctors had impressed on Charlie in particular how important it was that I use the thing multiple times a day and at least five times during each use. I despised it. Expanding my lungs was painful and I felt foolish, sucking on this silly plastic thingy that always showed me I wasn't measuring up. Charlie continued to remind me to the point that I began calling her Nurse Ratchet. Of course she was right in insisting I exercise my lungs; I did not develop any signs of pneumonia or other problems that can occur in post-op patients.

I kept record of my progress and, each day, I did manage to add 100 ml or so to my lung capacity. It took a full three weeks before I had gotten back to my pre-surgical volume and even then it was all I could do to draw in that much air.

Napping was a frequent occupation. I took at least two big naps each day, one in the morning and one in the afternoon, as well as several other cat-naps. My body clearly needed sleep.

The real problem was at night. While taking a nap in the recliner was easy, trying to sleep at night in the same position was devilishly difficult. I would lie awake for hours on end, trying not to toss and turn. Sometimes sleep just wouldn't come. One night I never slept at all; several other nights I would have to be satisfied with only an hour or two of sleep.

One night was particularly tough. I don't think I've ever had a panic attack, but I suspect it must be a lot like what I experienced. I couldn't sit still; I had to get up and pace. I was worried about everything. Another time I had managed to drift off to sleep when I woke up suddenly, completely overwhelmed by the magnitude of what had been done to me. The thought that my chest had been sawed apart and stretched open and that people had been inside there, handling my heart, was more than I could bear. The horror, the gruesome savagery of being cut open like that left me unable to cope. I felt like I was on a nightmarish rollercoaster ride that was becoming more and more violent as it reached the end of the track and plunged over the edge into a dark and endless abyss.

That was perhaps the lowest point in my recovery, and it happened unexpectedly after I had been home for more than a week. I wanted to document my feelings, not to frighten someone who might also go through a similar surgery or other traumatic procedure, but so that they won't be alarmed when or if it happens. Apparently such reactions are not uncommon. What gives me great comfort, however, is that I was able to pray, to ask the Lord to hold my hand as I experienced this disconnection from the moorings of sanity, and that He did just that. An hour later I realized that a vast sense of peace and calm pervaded my soul. The frenzied violence I had experienced was replaced by tranquility and confidence. The Lord was with me, of that I had no doubt.

Little by little, the bandages on my chest began to fall off. Patrick Pepper had told us to expect this. "Let them come off naturally," he said. "Don't rush them." Each shower found me a little stronger and more able to manage, and each time under the water teased the bandages off a bit more until, one day, they were clearly done.

Underneath was a site to behold. There were no visible stitches on my skin; instead the doctors had used what I can only describe as superglue to keep my various incisions in place. At first I thought that the scars would be very bumpy and frankly quite ugly. But I came to understand that most of the "bumps" were actually lumps of glue. The glue was stubborn. Like the bandages, Charlie and I let it slough off by itself without any encouragement from us. It took a full five weeks before the last of the glue was gone, leaving a remarkable set of wounds and scars behind.

It was as if a bird of prey with a spade-shaped beak had been given free rein to gouge out random chunks of flesh at its leisure. Incongruously, I was also struck with the notion that my chest represented a work of modern art. If I were to be displayed in an art museum, the description in the catalog might read something like this:

> The artist has used a human torso as his canvas, replete with age spots, freckles and other imperfections. Against a backdrop of sickly yellow and green gouache, the artist has worked an aggressive lightning bolt from top to bottom. This jarring slash is done with oils applied thickly with a pallet knife in reds, maroons, and crimsons. The work is finished off with what appear to be random bullet holes and other wounds. The artist describes his piece as a metaphor for the violence and divisions within our postmodern society.

The wounds on my chest were so remarkable that people who came to visit often wanted to see them. To be fair, I offered. Friends and family wanted to know about my ordeal; one very visual way to explain it was simply to unbutton my shirt and let them take a look. Most people were interested; a few were horrified. I hadn't meant to shock anyone and Charlie began to caution me that saying, "You wanna see my scar?" was probably not the most dignified way of interacting with well-wishers.

A number of people did come to see me in those first weeks home. Because the weather was so nice, I would often meet visitors on the porch. Meeting there also minimized catching some bug inadvertently. Given my delicate condition, catching something that would make me cough was to be avoided.

I also tried typing on a keyboard. I started trying to capture my recollections about the surgery. But the numbness in my two smallest fingers left me feeling like I had a couple of Vienna sausages tied to my hands. I was clumsy and constantly hitting the wrong keys.

The most important word for recovery from bypass surgery is patience. It simply takes time for such a major assault on a human body to heal. Patience had never been a strength of mine. In business, for example, if I saw something that needed to be done, I did it. "Never put off 'till tomorrow what you can do today" resonates strongly with me. I confess that efficiency had almost become a god to me. I liked results, and I liked them now.

So being patient through days, weeks and months of recovery was daunting. I had been forced to relinquish any activity related to my business. I couldn't do even the simplest task related to the garden or the flower beds. Preparing a Sunday School lesson was out of the question. The one thing I had going for me, if you can call it that, was that my stamina was almost nonexistent. I would try to do something, only to quickly run out of steam and have to stop. That alone prevented me from doing too much.

I sat in my recliner a lot, just gazing out the window at the blue sky, the puffy white clouds, at the goats grazing in the front pasture. I napped. I listened to music, although I found I didn't have the stamina to do much of that. I would often start listening to a playlist, only to doze off after just a few tracks had played.

I read a lot of books. I would read for a while, get drowsy, take a nap, then wake up bored and read some more. I started keeping track of the books I'd finished. It was quickly growing to be a long list. I read a fascinating biography of William Wilberforce by Eric Metaxas. I read three books by Francis Schaeffer. I read the complete *Basic Economics* by Thomas Sowell, all 700+ pages of it. I discovered David McCullough's *The Pioneers* about the settling of the "northwest territory," the place we today call Ohio. I read several romance novels by Rosamunde Pilcher, in my opinion the best writer in the genre. There were many more. Books helped instill the patience I needed.

I also renewed my interest in songbirds. I had always enjoyed identifying birds by their calls. A new app from Cornell University on my smart phone allowed me to listen to the birds that were singing and identify them with amazing accuracy. Charlie dug out our binoculars and suggested I use them to watch the birds, too. My ability to identify birds improved significantly during the long hours of sitting on the porch into late August and early September.

I learned to visually identify the onomatopoeically named Peewee. I also learned that it was a member of the Flycatcher family and I began to spot Great Crested Flycatchers as well. The highlight of my bird watching was the pair of Red Shouldered Hawks that would often go hunting together and the evenings when ten to twelve Nighthawks would approach high over the field in a squadron out looking for insects.

More friends came by to visit. The weather was beautiful in late August, so we would sit on the front porch and chat. After thirty minutes or less, I was just wiped out. Charlie learned to monitor my energy level and gently suggest that it was time to let me rest.

The number of people who wanted to come by for a visit touched me. Clearly I had caused some major consternation. After all, a man who is apparently healthy suddenly needing six heart bypasses is a bit shocking. I think it made all of us more cognizant of the fleeting nature of life. As a result, people did what we should all be doing: treating life and friendship as a precious gift, and doing something about it by getting together and sharing our love and concern for each other.

Lots of get well cards started arriving in the mail. Many were thoughtful and expressed concern, but several were humorous. I enjoyed those. One in particular came from a young man in our church. "In my family we don't quite know what to say when someone has a health issue," he wrote. "We tend to say, 'Just shake it off and get back to work.' So that's what I say to you: shake it off and get back to teaching Sunday School. We need you." Some may read that and say it was insensitive. I didn't take it that way at all. This person's love showed through with candor and a touch of comedy. I told him how much his card meant.

Each of the grandchildren came to see me within the first week. We sat on the porch and visited as long as my strength held out. It seemed they weren't quite sure what to say to their Pappaw who had been through this ordeal. I tried to set them at ease by being my old self, as much as I could, even though I couldn't really hug them or hold them on my lap.

One of the papers I was given during my interview with the "nurse on a stick" had to do with exercises. There were a series of activities I was to do at least twice a day along with increasing goals for walking.

The exercises were fairly simple. For example, I was to hold my arms in front of me and bend my elbows to bring my hands toward me. Each exercise was to be repeated ten times. Charlie began to do them with me. We would sit in chairs, facing each other, and go through the series of routines. Most of the exercises were not difficult, just tiring. One, however, was harder: I was to let my hands hang down at my sides, then lift them up so that my arms were straight out to the side and level with my shoulders. That exercise used muscles that the surgery had affected; it was quite painful to lift up my arms ten times. But each day got a little easier and we kept at it.

The first week I was to walk just five minutes, twice a day. That was fairly straight forward. A trip from the bedroom to the living room and back was almost enough.

The second week I was to increase the time to ten minutes. Because I craved sunshine and the weather was so beautiful, I began walking the length of the sidewalk across the front of our house. By the time I was into the fourth week I was making the trip all the way around the house, including down one set of steps and up another, and repeating that three times to get my time in.

By the time I was into the seventh week, I had to get more creative to get the right length in. I ended up walking down our rather long driveway twice. According to the app on my smartphone, I was up to walking about a half mile at a time.

My first doctor follow up visit was with Dr. Devers, two weeks after the surgery. I tried to express how grateful I was that he had listened to me about my shortness of breath episodes in Yellowstone. He was glad to see me doing so well.

I told him that my biggest problem was not being able to sleep. He prescribed a different pain medication and also a sleep aid. Unfortunately they didn't help much. The analgesic did not seem any more helpful that plain ibuprofen and the sleep aid made me feel very disoriented. With his concurrence, I discontinued both after just a few days.

Sleeping continued to be a problem and I got to the point that I really did resent the recliner, even though it was extremely comfortable. I just had a hard time sleeping only on my back. Charlie tried putting a pillow under my knees, which helped some. I was desperate for the day when I would be able to sleep in a bed. Meanwhile, I kept praying and trying to be patient.

After about four weeks I had an appointment to return to Dr. Dimeling's office for a follow up with the surgeon in Lexington. Charlie continued to be my chauffeur. I was told to first stop by the radiology department to get a chest Xray. The idea was to make sure no residual pneumonia was lurking. We arrived in Lexington at 8:00 AM and were first in line to get the Xray. Clearly several other patients were on a similar mission because they followed us in, one person in each pair clutching a doll's pillow to their chest. I had forgotten to bring mine because it didn't seem to do much good.

Once the Xray was complete, we headed to Dr. Dimeling's office. It was only a few short weeks since we had been there before, but it seemed an eternity ago. On that trip we knew that I might need surgery, but we had no idea of the extent or timing of the operation. Now, four weeks later, I had endured major surgery, had a big scar to prove it, and was struggling to gain back the basic functions of living.

Dr. Dimeling was gracious and pleased to see us. He said my chest Xray was clear and that I was progressing nicely. He again cautioned me that my heart was now in good shape with its rerouted plumbing; my major issue was allowing my sternum to knit back together properly. I was to continue to not lift anything over five pounds, but he did clear me to start driving. I wasn't sure I was ready for that, but it was good to know that I could.

"I'm releasing you," he told us. "I've done everything I need to do. You don't need to come back to see me any more unless you just want to. We have a bond, you and me. I've had my hands inside your chest cavity. If you ever just want to talk, make an appointment. I'd be glad to see you any time." He was right. There is some kind of bond between a doctor and a patient where the doctor has been that intimate with the patient's insides.

We thanked him for his God-given skill and for everything he'd done for us.

Before we left, I wanted to say hello to our nurse navigator, Debbie. She was in, and we had a good time of reconnecting. I think she was particularly pleased that a patient wanted to see her and thank her for her role in his recovery. She also was able to report that, indeed, the Missouri River is considered to be longer than the Mississippi.

On the way out I spotted a painting on the wall of the hallway. I had not noticed it the first time we had visited Dr. Dimeling, but it was particularly poignant to me now. I've since learned it is called *Chief of the Medical Staff* and was painted by an artist called Nathan Greene. It depicts an operating room with the surgeon and others around a patient undergoing open heart surgery, just like I had done. Among the monochromatic blues and greens of the physicians' scrubs and the drapes over the patient is one figure who stands out, almost glowing as He has one hand around the shoulder of the surgeon and, with the other hand, is guiding the surgeon's delicate work. The figure is clearly Jesus, ensuring that the surgery goes exactly as God has ordained it.

As the weeks slowly passed, I began to try to return to regular activities. Charlie and I went out to a restaurant for breakfast, something we had enjoyed doing before the surgery. I found I tired very easily, but I was able to manage. Everywhere we went, people were delighted to see us. In a small town news travels fast. It was common that people knew of our ordeal and were glad we were beginning to get back to normal.

A common comment after we had exchanged information about the surgery was, "Well, you really look good." I began to use a line my late father-in-law would have appreciated. "Hey," I would reply, "I have *always* looked good."

The first time back in church was surprisingly difficult. It was wonderful to be with my church family, but I barely had the stamina to sit in the pew for an hour. Trying to stand and sing hymns was more than I could manage. Several times during the first weeks I simply had to sit back down and just listen.

I was able to keep the appointment we'd made with Nancy to give me a haircut five weeks after the surgery.

Around seven weeks after the surgery we attended a special service at Jeremy Anderson's church. Before the service began, my cell phone rang. It was Debbie, the nurse navigator from Dr. Dimeling's office, just calling to check up on me. That was very impressive to me. She wanted to know what challenges I was having, how much exercise I was getting, how my vital signs were doing, and so on. I told her that I was slowly gaining strength and that I seemed to be doing as well as could be expected. "My biggest problem," I told Debbie, "is sleeping. I'm just no good at sleeping in a recliner."

"How long has it been since the surgery?" she asked.

I did some quick mental math. "Seven weeks today," I told her.

"Alright, then," she said. "Your sternum has healed enough that you can begin sleeping on your side. But pay attention to your body. It will tell you if sleeping on your side is uncomfortable. But, seven weeks out, you should be OK to sleep the way you're most comfortable. Besides, your body needs sleep to heal. Remember you still need to be careful with lifting."

It was the best news I could have gotten. I went into the church service feeling like a cloud had lifted.

It was around this time that I began trying to go to work for a bit. I found at first my brain couldn't handle more than about 30 minutes before I just gave out. Over the next month or so I began to be able to handle more, but my stamina took a long, long time to increase by tiny increments.

My numb fingers began to show signs that they might recover. It took a long time, but I began to be able to type again. I was very grateful for that; the inability to type would have been a significant disability for my line of work.

Soon after the call from Debbie I got a call from Jennifer who works at the cardiac rehabilitation facility in Richmond. The "nurse on a stick" had told me to expect a call like this, that cardiac rehab was a service offered to cardiac patients and paid for by insurance that would help me regain my stamina. I suggested to Jennifer that I should wait until I had my follow up visit with Dr. Cook, the cardiologist, which would be the coming Thursday, eight weeks after the original surgery.

Jennifer suggested I come in for an initial visit so that I could learn what cardiac rehab was all about and that way I could report to Dr. Cook, when I saw him, that I had begun the cardiac rehab process. I agreed to come in on Wednesday.

The cardiac rehab facility turned out to look a lot like a gym with plenty of exercise bikes, rowing machines, and the like, but with one major difference: there was a central desk where Jennifer and her colleague Rodney monitored the EKG and heart rate of each patient. Essentially, cardiac rehab meant going through increasingly challenging exercise routines with EKG leads on one's chest. These leads communicated wirelessly to the central console so Jennifer and Rodney could monitor how my heart was performing as I went through the workouts.

There were also be opportunities to attend classes with the hospital pharmacist regarding drugs most heart patients end up taking, and with the hospital head dietitian about how to adjust one's diet to be more heart healthy.

Jennifer and Rodney wanted to hear my story and began to formulate a strategy for my particular situation. I learned how to place the EKG leads on my chest and Rodney showed me the machines he thought would be best for me to exercise on. Thus began what would become a three day a week routine that involved driving to Richmond and spending about an hour and fifteen minutes on various exercise devices, accompanied by the encouragement of my new friends. With travel, each visit ended up taking almost a half day to complete, but that was OK; I was still not nearly ready to return to work full time.

The follow-up appointment with Dr. Cook arrived. I came to him with a big list of questions. By now I had been recovering for eight weeks and there were things I wanted to know. For example, I wanted to know about basic activities I might consider starting to do again. Dr. Cook said he would raise my weight limit to 30 pounds now instead of the five pound limit under which I had been operating. That was a major improvement, but it still meant that lifting a 50 pound sack of goat feed was not something I should be doing. Chopping firewood was out of the question. But other activities could be resumed, as long as I listened to my body and didn't overdo it.

We reviewed my medication and Dr. Cook was very good to explain the purpose of each one and to also note which ones we might consider stopping at some point in the future. "Some of these you'll probably be on for the rest of your life," he said. "But others we might think about stopping after a year."

I asked if I would continue seeing him. He chuckled. "Yes, I'm afraid you're kind of stuck with me," he said. "After what you've been through, you're going to want to visit a cardiologist once a year. I think you'll have me for the duration."

Dr. Cook was also good to give me a more detailed picture of what was done inside my chest. He pointed out the anomalous configuration of my cardiac arteries and where the blockages were that made it necessary to do six bypasses. We left the visit with our questions answered and with me committing to go through the cardiac rehab program.

With Dr. Cook's concurrence, I began meeting cousin John to go walking on the two weekdays I was not going in for cardiac rehab. I also began teaching Sunday School again. And I started going into the office more.

As I write this it has now been four full months since the surgery. In another few weeks I will have completed my 36 visits to the cardiac rehab facility. I'm still not back to pre-surgery normal, but I do have a new normal that is working fairly well. I'm beginning to understand what many people have told me, that it really does take a full year to completely recover from surgery of this magnitude. The patience that was so necessary for the first two months continues to be required now as well.

Opportunity

Some years ago I was attending a dinner with a group of faculty at a small college in North Carolina. I found myself sitting next to a professor who taught in the Education department. She mentioned that she attended a Unitarian church.

"Oh?" I said. "Tell me more about that. I don't know much about Unitarians. What do Unitarians believe?"

"We don't believe anything specifically," she replied. "With us, people are free to believe whatever they like." I took this to mean that Unitarians do not espouse a particular creed or theology. This was fascinating to me, and I wondered how far it went.

"That's really interesting," I said. "So the Unitarian church would be comfortable with a person who believed that, when they died, they would go to Heaven."

"Yes, of course."

"But you'd also be supportive of a person who believed that, when they died, they would simply cease to exist and that their body would return to the earth."

"Yes ..."

"And the Unitarians would also accept someone who believed that, when they died, they would be reincarnated and live another life as another person or perhaps as an animal."

"Well, yes. Because we don't try to impose our beliefs on anyone ..."

"Tell me," I asked. "When a person dies, what does happens to them? Does what they believe actually affect what happens after they die? For example, does the person who believes they will go to Heaven actually go to Heaven? And does the person who believes they will cease to exist just do that? And does the person who believes in reincarnation get reborn as someone else?"

"Well ...". She was struggling. I had placed her in an indefensible position. Could it be possible that believing something to be true would make it so? "Well ... we aren't judgmental. We're very tolerant ..."

"I'm sure you are," I replied. "But I'm really impressed with you Unitarians. It seems to me you have incredible power. Each one of you can control reality based on whatever you believe. You are able to bend the cosmos to your own will. That's amazing to me."

At this point the conversation ground to a halt and she turned to talk to her neighbor on the other side. Frankly, there was no answer to my questions. Of course Unitarians don't have that kind of power over life and death. No one does. But they have, in their quest for tolerance, thrown the baby out with the bathwater. They say you can believe whatever you want, but they fail to recognize *believing does not make it so.*

I may believe fervently that I can fly, but that doesn't mean I can. Many things — including my inability to fly — are true, regardless of what I may or may not think about them. I can climb on the roof of my house, continuing in my fervent belief, and jump off. I can believe I can fly right up to the instant I hit the ground. No amount of wishing or believing will make something true that is not true, nor will it make something untrue if it is actually the truth.

Rather than saying, "I believe this" or "I believe that," the Unitarians and all the rest of us would do so much better recognizing that there is Truth that is out there. I may be way off in my understanding of it, and you may be closer to it than I am, but neither of us can modify or nullify the Truth. Regardless of what we think, the Truth is still the Truth. We would all do well to seek after it.

The Northwest Portico of the Jefferson memorial quotes Thomas Jefferson when he was Secretary of State. Jefferson said, "Almighty God hath created the mind free." In reacting to that statement, Christopher Flannery said[1] that "this freedom of mind equips and therefore obliges us to seek the truth that we should be guided by—that all nobility, all that is worthwhile in life, depends on finding this truth and living by it, and failing to seek it with all our heart, mind, and soul is to let our lives slip through our fingers like water."

That has been my quest as I have experienced events surrounding my CABG open heart surgery. I want to learn aspects of the Truth as uncovered in my journey. I want to be diligently searching for Truth rather than making up my own little truths as I go along.

So what do I make of what has happened to me? What aspects of the Truth have I discovered? What lessons have I learned? During my convalescence I've had time to think about this. A lot of time. What I've found has been the main reason for writing this little book.

I have a hope that the details of what I experienced may be helpful to you, particularly if you are facing or are newly recovering from some kind of life-altering event. Even if the person going through major surgery is not you, but

---

[1] Flannery, Christopher, "American Christmas, American New Year," <u>Imprimis</u>, Volume 51, Number 12, December 2022, p. 5.

someone you love, my journey may help you understand their experience. I hope I have been transparent enough so that you can feel, with some clarity, the challenges — physical, mental, emotional, and spiritual — that accompanied my ordeal. I also hope that I have not been too candid, including details that might offend your sensibilities.

Most importantly, however, I would like to offer these four thoughts. So far as I can discern, these seem to be aspects of the eternal Truth that have become evident to me during this ordeal. I offer them in the hopes that they may be helpful. They may seem a bit trite, yet they are so fundamentally True that they bear repeating. These basic principles are particularly meaningful to me now in the wake of my surgery.

Be Ready to Go

It is self-evident that everyone dies. Some of us live a very long time. Others' lives are cut short through accident, disease, and other traumas. Regardless of its length, life does eventually end. In an attempt to prolong our lives we may become extremely risk adverse. We may take vitamins and supplements, make a religion of exercise, or latch on to every medical advancement, all for the same reason. In the end, however, the dust reclaims us.

I've often wondered if, given the choice, would people want to know the hour of their passing? We might think that knowing would help us to plan and use the time we have better. But what would you do as the day approaches? It sounds terrifying to me to know that date you have circled on the calendar in red will be your last. It would make life like unto that of a condemned man. No, better not to know.

Still, even if we don't know, we do know that the day will come. For me, lying on the gurney in pre-op, waiting to be wheeled back to surgery, knowing that my chest would be opened up and my very life exposed, was to stare death in the face. I was under no illusions about the future. August 5 could very well have been my day circled in red.

I did not find myself fighting against the riptide of time. Instead, I found myself at peace. I was going to meet my destiny, a destiny I did not know, but one that I could trust. I knew, and know, Who holds my life in His hands. It wasn't the doctors or the technicians or the nurses. It was no less than the Lord Himself, and His timing is the right timing, whether it was August 5 or many decades from now.

Some people may marvel at my equanimity. How could I be so calm? My answer is a simple word, but one that requires some explanation. The simple word is faith. The explanation is that my faith isn't a "hope so, toss the dice and maybe I'll get lucky" kind of faith. It is a faith borne of experience, observation and study. Faith doesn't have to be a coin toss; it can be grounded much more deeply than that. For example, I have faith that the sun will come up tomorrow. I could be wrong; it may not come up after all. But experience, observation and study have driven me to conclude that the sun will come up, even though it hasn't happened yet.

My faith in God is that kind of faith. I have experienced His love and his care for me. I have observed how He works in people's lives, including mine. I have studied what He has determined to reveal to us about Himself. I am confident in Him, even if some of the things about which I am confident have yet to happen.

That kind of faith is what allowed me to be in that pre-op room, stare death in the face, and not blink.

The Bible tells us that "to be absent from the body is to be present with the Lord." (2 Corinthians 5:8). Jesus told us that He would go to prepare a place for us. He added, "If I go and prepare a place for you, I will come again, and receive you unto myself; that where I am, there you may be also." (John 14:2-3) I have no doubt that, had I died on the operating table, I would have been with Jesus. The scripture that had come to me when I first found out I needed bypass surgery sustained me: Jesus said (John 11:25), "I am the resurrection, and the life: he that believeth in me, though he were dead, yet shall he live."

This was the first thing that came home to me during my journey through this surgery: you have to be ready to go. Every one of us could go at any time. You don't have to be facing major surgery and peering through the thin gauze that separates life on earth from eternity. You could simply be driving your car, not knowing about the truck coming toward you with failed brakes. You could unknowingly be harboring cancer cells in your body that will take you within the year. A tornado could be brewing a hundred miles away that will take your home and your life as well. Not being ready to go is foolish, for we will all die at some point. I simply had the advantage of coming a little closer to the portal than many people do; I looked at death and was prepared.

How did I get the kind of faith that allowed me to be ready to go? The answer is deceptively simple.

First, however, let's be clear: I do not claim to know all of the Truth. I am still searching for a deeper understanding of it. But in my finite, limited way I have come to have faith, the kind of know-so faith that believes the sun will come up tomorrow, that believes God loves me and cares for me, that believes God wants the very best for me. The simple children's song has a profound truth in it: "Jesus loves me, this I know, for the Bible tells me so."

With that kind of faith, we can echo the Apostle Paul's words to the Corinthians, "Where, O death, is your victory? Where, O death, is your sting?" (I Corinthians 15:55) His words have a hint of mockery. Death has lost its power, lost its terror. If you know where you're going, death is but a journey, not a calamity.

Can you be certain of your destination? Absolutely yes! The Bible tells us "If you declare with your mouth, 'Jesus is Lord,' and believe in your heart that God raised him from the dead, you will be saved." (Romans 10:9). In other words, if you believe in your heart that God raised the crucified Jesus out of His burial place — demonstrating His victory over death — and are willing to tell others of your faith, that's all it takes. There is no magic formula you must recite, no special mission you must undertake, no complex ritual to perform. All it takes is simple belief, simple faith. No more than that.

But notice that it also takes no less than that. You can't just say you believe, but have your fingers crossed behind your back when you say it. You simply can't recite the words without having faith that they are true. That kind of gamesmanship won't save you.

Simple faith is what it takes.

When I first received the news from Dr. Cook, the cardiologist, that I needed major surgery and I needed it now, and then when that diagnosis was confirmed by the surgeon, Dr. Dimeling, I had to do some major soul searching. Was I really ready to go? I had only five days between the meeting with the surgeon and my date with his scalpel. Five days to determine if my faith was genuine or just lip service.

I knew, lying on that operating table, chatting glibly with the anesthesiologist about what small world it was, that, if this was it, I would be welcomed into the throne room of Heaven, and that I would be glad to go. You can know that, too. And that, my friend, is the first big lesson from my surgical ordeal: make sure you are ready to go.

Make the Most of Every Day

According to Wikipedia, right now the oldest person alive is a woman living in France. She is 118 years old. There isn't anyone older than that, which means that, regardless of what we do, we're not likely to live more than roughly 120 years. Some of us — and I count my pre-surgical self in that category — are likely to fall many years short of that when we do pass on.

Living 120 years may seem like a long time. Yet at my age, life seems to be hurtling by at faster and faster speeds. The biblical statement that "life is but a vapor" rings true. I grew up in the mountains of western North Carolina. It was common for fog to form in the early hours of the morning. Often the fog was very thick, reducing visibility to near zero. It was common for folks to observe, "It'll burn off soon." To say that the fog would burn off meant that the sun's warmth would soon dissipate the fog — and that's exactly what would happen, time after time. In the Appalachian mountains, we understood that the vapor of fog doesn't last long. It is here for a a little while, and then it is gone.

Life is like that. When we're young we may feel invincible, but I imagine you know of several young people that were tragically taken by an accident. When we're older, we know that death is nearer now than it once was. Life is indeed like a vapor.

My point is simply that, no matter how long your life ends up being, time is short. Every day you do have is a gift. You should treat it like that and make the most of every day.

What does it look like to make the most of every day? One thing that is hard is knowing that, while today may indeed be our last day, more than likely we have many years left. We have to balance the immediate present with the longer future. If we knew we would die tomorrow, we wouldn't invest in any long term projects. We wouldn't put money away for retirement. We wouldn't worry about paying off our mortgage. We wouldn't worry about getting together with friends we wouldn't ever see again. But those are all good things. Making the most of every day does not mean ignoring the future.

In fact, making the most of every day means including future plans in what you do today. It means that every word and every action should not be something you'll regret or have to go back and fix later. What you do today should not cause regret or remorse in the future.

You may have heard this trope: no one, on their death bed, says "I wish I'd gone to work more." People use this aphorism to focus on work/life balance, or even to justify laziness. It does contain some truth, however. Thinking about the end of one's life and what you might wish you had done differently is just the thing needed to make some adjustments today. Do you imagine you might wish you had stayed in touch with an old friend more frequently? Why not reach out to them today? Do you know there is something you've done that caused hurt to someone you care about? Today would be a good day to apologize and make it right. Do you think sometimes that your work consumes you? How about making this the day you leave work a little early instead of staying the usual two hours overtime. Have you taken your spouse for granted? This would be a good time to go the extra mile to let your spouse know how important they are to you.

Since we know our time is limited, it may be helpful to think about what we might hope people would say at our funeral. If people are going to be able to say truthfully nice things about you when you die, what changes do you need to make today so that, when the end does come, those nice things will be true?

While I was waiting in pre-op the morning of the surgery, Mark asked me, "Dad, you really don't have any regrets, do you?" That's what he was talking about. There are many things I've done that I'm not proud of, but so far as was possible, I have tried to make peace with those around me, to express love to those in my path, and to live a life of integrity.

We could go another step and say that we should avoid doing things that we'll have to repent of later. I myself have found that God's intended way for people to live is by far the best. Following God's design for our lives is the surest way I know to avoid regret and grief.

Unfortunately, we prefer to go our own way and do our own thing. Often we do so at our peril. God has provided us clear instructions for living. I will admit that some of it is extremely challenging. Ultimately, however, God's way of making the most of every day is far and away the best way.

As I was facing surgery, I kept coming back to the verse from 1 Thessalonians 5:19. As I was having to make the wrenching change in a very short time from blissful ignorance to having my chest cut open and my cardiac plumbing rerouted, the words "Quench not the Spirit" frequently came to mind. The Spirit referred to here is the Holy Spirit, that aspect of God that He imparts to us, once we have made the commitment to make Jesus our Lord and Savior. To quench the Spirit would be to ignore God's quiet invitation. It would be like dousing a burning log with water. Instead of providing warmth and light, it becomes a soggy mess. To make the most of every day, I needed to be better tuned to the leading of the Holy Spirit. It was the Spirit that led me to spend extra time on the treadmill during the stress test. It was the Sprit that led me to agree to the heart catheterization procedure. It was the Spirit that led me to select Dr. Dimeling as my surgeon. It was the Sprit that led me to talk with Thomas from housekeeping.

To make the most of every day, we have to be tuned to the Holy Spirit's leading. That takes practice and attention. It means tuning out our own selfishness and our own wants.

I don't have a lot of knick-knacks on the desk in my office. Clutter in front of me, I've found, leads to clutter in my mind and in how I work. I prefer to keep focused and organized.

However, I do have one quote taped on the monitor of my computer. Helen Keller said, "I long to accomplish a great and noble task, but it is my chief duty to accomplish small tasks as if they were great and noble." That really resonates with me.

The words of this woman, who was deaf and blind, see right into the longing of my soul. I long to do something memorable, something that will be noticed, something "great and noble." Yet it seems that, in order to make the most of every day, I must do the mundane, the routine, the ordinary in the same way that a great and noble task would be done.

That, I think, is the key: it is to do the ordinary things of life with integrity, following the leading of the Holy Spirit. Then, when your time comes, as it almost did for me, you will not be found wanting. You will be found with no regrets and no guilt.

Treat Folks Around You Right

The Bible gives an account of a lawyer who came to Jesus and asked what he had to do to achieve eternal life. We learn from reading the story that this man was secretly arrogant. He thought he had it all figured out, but he wanted to justify himself to this rabbi who was teaching about the Kingdom of God.

Jesus's response was interesting. As He so often did, He answered the lawyer's question with a question of His own. He asked, "What is written in the law?" In other words, what does the Bible tell you you should do? The Torah or Old Testament contained God's instructions for living; this lawyer should have known well what was written there.

He responded with the standard answer, that we are to love God with everything we have and we are to love our neighbor as much as we love ourselves. Jesus responded, "You have answered correctly. Do that, and you shall live."

But the lawyer wasn't content to leave it there. He assumed he was already doing both things, so he pushed back on Jesus's answer, asking "And who is my neighbor?"

Again, Jesus did not give a straight answer, but instead told the story we call the Parable of the Good Samaritan. You may know the account. If you don't, be sure and read it in Luke 10:25-37. Jesus told about a man who was mugged as he traveled and left for dead on the side of the road. Two different religious people walked past him and didn't help, but a man from Samaria did stop. This was particularly significant because the Jews and the Samaritans supposedly did not get along, much as we are told different "races" do not get along today.

Jesus asked the lawyer which of the three people, the two religious people and the Samaritan man, had treated the beaten man like a neighbor. The lawyer again answered correctly, saying that the Samaritan had been the neighbor.

Jesus simply said, "Go and do the same thing."

Every day we interact with people who are right in front of us. Some of those are people we know well: our spouse, our family, our coworkers, our classmates. Some of them are chance encounters: a waitress at a restaurant, a man filling up his car with gas at the next pump, a lady mailing a package at the post office. According to the Parable of the Good Samaritan, these are all people who we should think of as our neighbors.

We worry a lot about people that are far, far away. During my convalescence there were devastating floods in eastern Kentucky that left many people homeless. There is a war going on in Ukraine in which Russia seems determined to bomb the country to smithereens. There was a murder of four college students in Idaho; so far there are few leads as to who might have done this tragic crime. I could go on and on. My point is that, as compassionate and upset as we may be about these things, are they taking our focus away from the neighbor who is right in front of us?

It seems to me it is part of our sinful human nature to fret and stew about things over which we can have little influence, and ignore the people who are in our immediate path. Perhaps we do this because focusing on the neighbor in front of us would require us to do something, to get our hands dirty, to get involved. As long as we can piously worry about things far away, we give the appearance of being pious without needing to do anything.

That doesn't cut it. We need to treat the folks who are around us right.

The problem is that the people in front of us are complicated, they come with baggage, we might have some unpleasant history we would have to overcome, they might smell bad or look funny. That shouldn't matter.

I met a lot of people before and after my surgery: nurses and doctors, physical therapists and respiratory therapists, housekeeping people and folks from the cafeteria, visitors and nurses aides. Every single one of them became, for that time, my neighbor. I needed to treat them right, even though I was the one who was scared to death, even though I was the one in serious pain.

There can be different reasons for treating people right, but none is more compelling than the reason the Bible provides. According to Genesis 1, God made all human beings in His own image. That means every person, from the most exalted celebrity to the homeless man asking for money on a street corner, bears the image of God. There is something special about each person because of Who made them, not because of what they have done or how charming or good looking they are.

The other reasons for treating people right begin to fall apart if you push them hard enough. If you believe that people should be judged based on their wealth or achievements or looks, or if you do not see people as the image bearers of God, it becomes easy to discount some individuals. The minute we start doing that we have started down a path that winds up with some people being marginalized, despised and seen as unworthy.

The Truth is that every life counts, every life is worthy of respect because it bears the image of God. The Truth is that we should love our neighbors as ourselves.

Years ago I read a book initially published in 1936. Dale Carnegie's *How to Win Friends and Influence People* seems perhaps a little old fashioned to our modern sensibilities. But the ideas it contains really help us to see the person in front of us as our neighbor and worthy of respect.

Carnegie's main point is that everyone has a story to tell about themselves, and every one of those stories is interesting and worth hearing. You can win a lot of friends if you will simply be interested in learning more about them and finding common ground.

As I interacted with people at the hospital, I tried to learn their names. Many wore badges indicating their name, which made that easy. I tried to remember and use those names when talking. I usually would ask where they were from; I've found that's an easy question because everyone is from somewhere. That conversation would often lead to other discussions; it doesn't take long to find things you have in common with every person you meet. Investing in those relationships is both the right thing to do and a rewarding thing to do.

I have the opinion that one of the best gifts God gives us here on Earth are the friendships we form. The relationships between people are a reflection of the relationship God desires to have with us. Friendships are a foretaste of the joys that come from knowing and being known, of loving and being loved.

I can't leave the topic of treating folks right without also pointing out that I was the recipient of that gift. Folks in the hospital were mostly very caring and wanted the best for me. I am deeply appreciative of that.

None, however, can match the love and care I received from my wife. Her husband was swiftly taken from her and severely incapacitated. The days in the hospital, followed by two months of intense recovery, were tough on her. Yet Charlie was single-mindedly dedicated to my well-being. If every anyone was treated right, it was me, under the ministry of my wife's healing care.

Get On Board with God's Assignments

If you're with me so far regarding the things I learned from my experience of having my CABG heart re-plumbed, then I have one final observation for you. If being ready to go makes sense to you, and if you see it is important to make the most of every day, and if you agree we need to treat the folks around us right, then maybe this will make sense as well. If you're not on board with the first three, you might want to skip this one because it is the least specific.

The final learning is that we need to be prepared to get on board with God's assignments. Here's how I came to that conclusion.

According to the doctors, I would not have survived an "event." My heart was a ticking time bomb. I was one of those men who would prematurely have died while shaving or mowing the yard or just going about life. The fact that Dr. Cook, the cardiologist, wanted me to go home and rest in a recliner while he lined up a surgeon to do the surgery, and the fact that Dr. Dimeling, the surgeon, wanted me not to even do something as simple as walking for exercise, told me a lot. These medical professionals felt urgently that my time was very limited unless something was done.

Further, there were a whole series of events that led up to the surgery that apparently had saved my life. Had I not hiked in Yellowstone and paid attention to being short of breath, had I not mentioned that to Dr. Devers, my regular doctor, had he not listened and asked me to have a stress test, had I not gone further on the treadmill during the stress test than was needed, had Dr. Cook not recommended a heart cath procedure, had I not agreed to the heart cath (that's the one where Charlie most clearly sees the hand of God — I never easily agree to any medical procedure), had Dr. Dimeling not decided to practice his particular brand of CABG surgery in Lexington, had any one of a thousand things that could have gone wrong during the surgery gone sideways, I would likely not be writing this and, instead, you might have been attending my funeral. But that isn't what happened.

You may not agree with me, but I clearly see the hand of God in all of this. God orchestrated an extensive series of events so that I might have a successful surgery and be alive today to tell about it.

Thoughts like that cause me to pause and think. First they make me grateful, despite being ready to go. Second, and of particular importance to this point, they make me wonder why. Why did God ordain that I would have this surgery instead of dying? For what purpose did God protect me?

※

I titled this final chapter "Opportunity." The whole experience was an opportunity to learn key Truths in a very concrete and visceral way. More than that, it is clear to me that I went through the surgery and recovery for a purpose. That purpose is my big opportunity. As I write this I am eagerly waiting, (and trying to be patient about it), to learn what God has in store for me. Instead of dying soon, unless God has other plans, I am likely to have decades more in which to do something. The question is, what? Therein lies the opportunity.

Having serious major surgery gave me the opportunity to experience, in intimate and tangible ways, the preciousness of life. Every life, yours and mine, is a gift. Whether we have days or decades, we need to be using them wisely. If we're not ready to go, we need to prepare by knowing God personally. We need to make the most of every day we have. We need to be treating everyone around us right. And we need to be asking God, listening to His Spirit, discerning what assignment He has for us. For some of us, this may mean a dramatic shift in career or location or lifestyle. For others it may mean an assurance that we should keep doing what we are doing as if it is a great and noble task, even though it may not seem so to us.

Are you a mother raising children? I can think of no higher calling. Do you share what you have learned with others in some kind of teaching ministry? What a beneficial thing to be doing. Do you provide service to others through your work, through volunteering, or through other means? Well done! Are you married and dedicated to loving and serving your spouse? Your marriage is the building block of society.

We each need to be asking, "What is God asking me to do?" When we receive the answer, we need to be ready to get on board with that assignment. We need to be like Peter and Andrew, James and John; when Jesus invited them to "Follow me!" they left their fishing nets and did just that. Jesus once asked Peter about his commitment to following the Lord (John 6:68). Several others had appeared to be ready to get on board with Jesus' assignment, but their commitment turned out to be shallow. Jesus asked Peter if he, too, would be leaving. Peter's reply is what I want my reply to be: "Where else would we go? You have the words of eternal life."

There really is only one assignment worth getting on board with, and that is the assignment being given you by God. God got my attention rather dramatically with sextuple bypass surgery. I strongly feel I've been shown that I have a new opportunity, and I'm waiting to discern my new orders.

Even without major surgery, you, too, have an opportunity to heed to God's calling. I hope you will take your opportunity, just as I am taking mine, to know it and to run with it.

www.ingramcontent.com/pod-product-compliance
Lightning Source LLC
Chambersburg PA
CBHW060816050426
42449CB00008B/1680